D1221940

The First Book of Tools

The FIRST BOOK of TOOLS

The Story of the 12 Tools of Man

by GENE LIBERTY

Pictures by Richard Mayhew

FRANKLIN WATTS, INC.
575 LEXINGTON AVENUE • NEW YORK 22

For Rose and Unc

5

Library of Congress Catalog Number: 60-5578

Printed in the United States of America
by Polygraphic Company of America, Inc.

CONTENTS

Life in the Old Stone Age 11
The Wonder of the Human Hand 14
The Meaning of Tools 16
The 12 Tools of Man 17
Six Simple Machines 24
Is It Work or Wasted Effort? 24
Pulleys 26
The Law of Work 28
Friction Uses up Force 28
The Lever 28
The Wheel and Axle 31
The Inclined Plane 31
The Wedge 33
The Screw 34
The Wheel and Other Moving Circles 34
The Discovery of Tools 37
A Prehistoric Story 38
Stone, Wood, and Bone 39
Growing and Grinding 43
The Coming of Metals 49
From Generation to Generation 53
Special Words 56
Index 59

Life in the Old Stone Age

THE FIRST humans lived in the forest. They did not know how to talk, nor did they have fire or tools. When they dug for roots to eat, caught game, moved things or tore anything apart, they used their hands and teeth. Most of their time was spent in a never-ending search for food, warmth, and safety. Without the help of tools, these early men could only rely on their slow, still-undeveloped brains and their strong bodies to survive.

It was a million years ago, during a period of distant history called the Old Stone Age. Man was new in the world. His ancestors had been tree dwellers, and he was just learning to make the ground his home. He lived like the animals he hunted and feared.

Picture early man — apparently defenseless — and surrounded by powerful animals that move at great speeds, striking with savage claws, long teeth, sharp tusks, pointed horns, or slashing talons.

The weather was often a bitter enemy. Bare skin was a thin shield against the rain, the sun, and the wind. When winter came, early man lacked the thick coat of hair of the sheep or bear to protect him from the snow and cold. Unarmed and unclothed, early man seemed to have a poor chance to survive.

Yet he fought the greatest fight for life that the world has known. It lasted hundreds of thousands of years. There were times when he was helped by nature, and times when nature was against him. The forest yielded fruits, insects, roots, and small game, but it also concealed the saber-toothed tiger. The river where early man caught fish was also the lair of the man-eating crocodile. The cave that offered shelter could hide a hyena or bear. The wind that cooled him might carry his scent to animals and reveal his position.

The sun that warmed him frequently burned his skin and dried up his water hole.

But man persisted. From the tropics to the arctic, he conquered his environment. Man has never been defeated by claws, the superior muscles and swiftness of his aggressors, or the hardships of nature. His brain gives him greater strength than all of these. Within man's brain there is a remarkable power to feel, to reason, to plan, and to invent.

He has the ability to look at a rough object and then picture in his mind what he will make of it. A rock, for example, will become a hammer; a branch, a handle; an animal bone, a knife. Man can also think about things that are not material objects at all, such as courage, truth, or humor. No other animal except man has this imagination and high intelligence.

Some animals can pick up objects found in nature, like pebbles, twigs, or stones, and use them as tools. Yet these animals never make new tools nor do they try to improve the natural shapes that they find. Among all the animals, only man invents tools to make his work easier. Man alone can learn from the present and the past, and then use his information to explore the future.

Animals use tools, too. If the otter finds a shellfish with a very hard shell, he finds a flat rock to use as an anvil. Putting the rock on his chest, he smashes the shellfish down hard to open it.

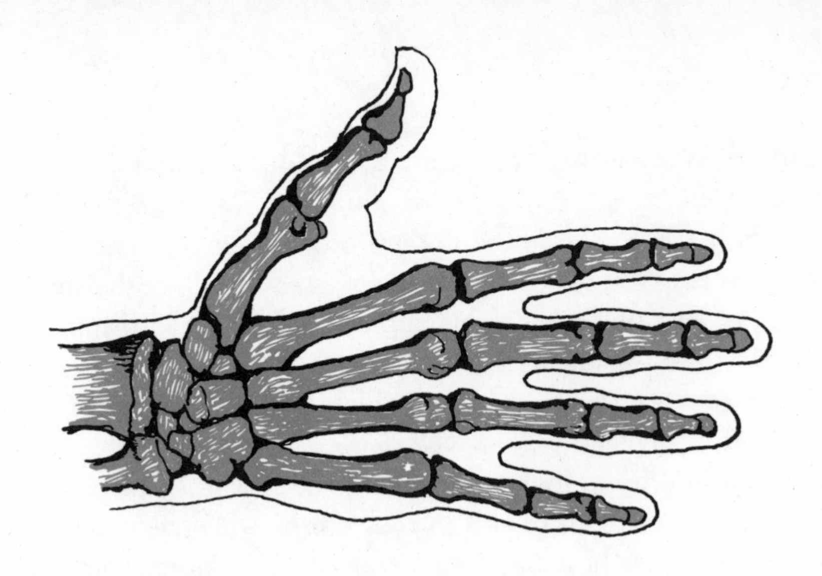

The Wonder of the Human Hand

MAN'S success in shaping and using tools is, in part, a tribute to the remarkable construction of his hands. After he began to live on the ground, man no longer needed his hands to carry him through the trees that were once his home. He was now able to travel on his feet leaving his hands free for other work. It would take him thousands of years, but he would learn what truly marvelous instruments they are for holding and wielding objects.

Most of the jobs that the human hand can do depend on the thumb. This broad fifth finger is strong. It also has the ability to press against the other fingers. Without this pressure between the thumb and one or more of the other fingers, it would be difficult to hold onto anything.

Here is a simple test that will show why the thumb is man's most important finger. Pick up a pencil without using your thumb. Write the sentence that you have just read. Do not let the thumb touch the pencil. After you have finished put the pencil down.

Then pick it up again, this time using your thumb as you normally do, and rewrite the sentence. It is easy to see how the thumb enables you to grasp the pencil firmly and control its movement.

The hand and all of its fingers closes and opens and moves freely. No machine has ever been built that can exactly duplicate this astonishing flexibility. "And the narrowest hinge in my hand," the poet Walt Whitman wrote, "puts to scorn all machinery."

Notice, too, that the palm of the hand and the insides of the fingers are padded like cushions. If you look at a pencil held between the tip of your thumb and the tip of your first finger, you can see how the soft pads of the fingers help to grip an object by taking its shape.

Try holding a small box in place of the pencil. Instead of curving, your fingertips will flatten out. They will fit as snugly against the flat surface of the box as they did on the round curve of the pencil.

The pencil and the box are held by the pressure of your two fingers pushing together. More pressure would be needed were it not for the tiny ridges and valleys that make up the fingerprints.

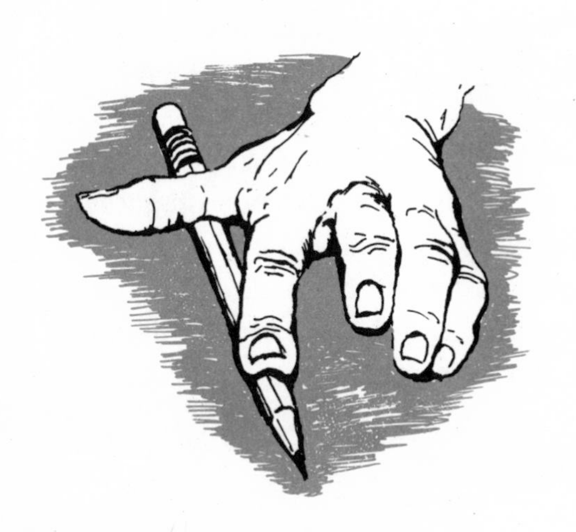

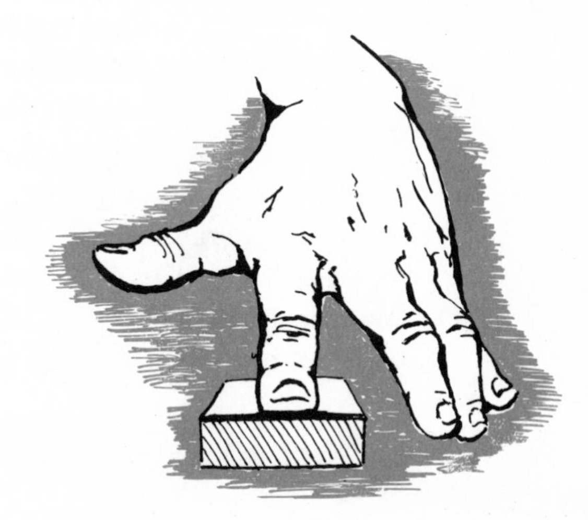

These high and low spots help to prevent slipping, even when holding very smooth objects.

The fingertips are also very sensitive. When you touch something, the many nerve endings in your fingertips signal your brain. You know immediately whether the object you are touching is hot or cold, soft or hard, smooth or rough, flat or round.

The hand, with its delicate sense of touch and its ability to perform skilled wonders, works in close cooperation with the eye and the brain. Although man's two eyes see separately, he is one of the few animals whose brain combines the two pictures that it receives into a single picture. With some exceptions, like the apes and several monkeys, other animals see two different pictures. The single picture that man sees has depth instead of being flat.

With eyes that could gauge distances and depths, hands that could perform skillful work, and a brain to direct him, it was natural for man to become a toolmaker.

The Meaning of Tools

ALTHOUGH everyone uses tools, the word itself has different meanings for different people. It is rarely defined very exactly. In general we say that tools are simple instruments for doing work. They are like detachable parts of the body that can be used and then put aside until they are needed again.

A machine is a more complicated device than a tool. The energy to operate a tool is supplied by the body. If a device is operated by outside energy, like electricity, gasoline, or atomic power, it is not regarded as a tool. In everyday language we call this a machine, or *power tool.* A hand saw, for example, is a tool, while an electric table saw is referred to as a machine.

There are six inventions, among them the lever and the wedge, that are described by scientists as *simple machines.* Later on, we shall see how most tools are combinations or variations of the six simple machines.

All tools extend, or broaden, the use of different organs of the body — especially the hands and the teeth. For example, man can dig with his hands, but he can dig much better with a shovel or a spade. He can also cut far more efficiently with a knife or a saw. He can use both his hands and his teeth for attack or defense, but he will be more successful using an axe, a knife, or a spear — weapons that increase the reach of his hands and deepen the bite of his teeth. Such weapons are also regarded as tools. They are simple extensions of the body, designed for the special work of fighting and hunting.

The 12 Tools of Man

THERE are thousands of special tools made in the modern world. Files alone can be bought in 3000 separate kinds and sizes. All 3000 files, however, are used for the same general purpose — to scrape surfaces smooth. So are sandpaper and chisels. Though there are hundreds of different hammers, each one of them is used for a similar job — pounding. Axes and knives also are used for an almost identical chore — cutting.

Look carefully at the next pages and you will see that all special tools can be divided into 12 groups. The tools that belong to a single group all perform similar work or operate on the same principle. Because of the variety of new tools that are constantly made, each group continues to grow. Yet for thousands of years

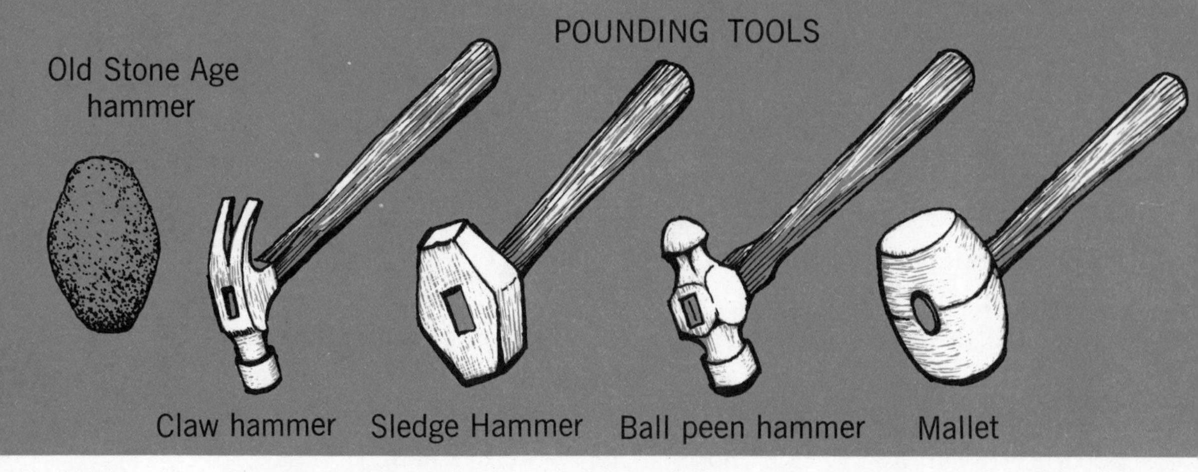

CLAW HAMMER: for driving nails in general carpentry work

SLEDGE HAMMER: for heavy or rough pounding

BALL PEEN HAMMER: for metal working

MALLET: for pounding soft materials

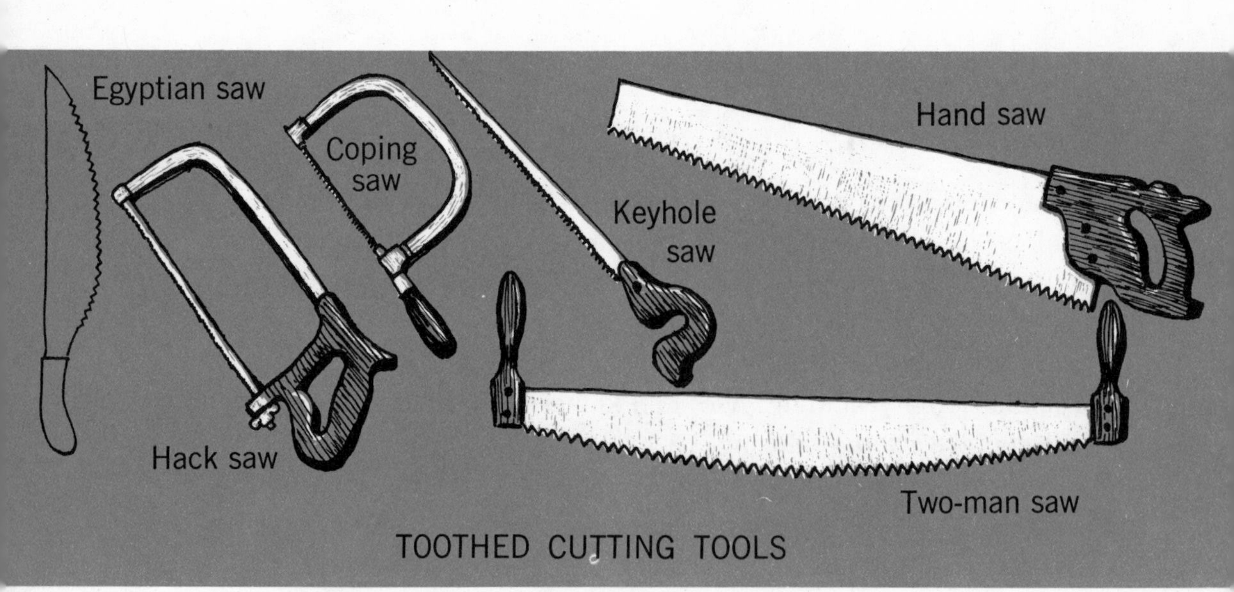

HACK SAW: for cutting metals

COPING SAW: for shaping fine curves in wood

KEYHOLE SAW: for shaping rough curves in wood

HAND SAW: for cutting straight wooden edges

TWO-MAN SAW: for cutting trees and logs

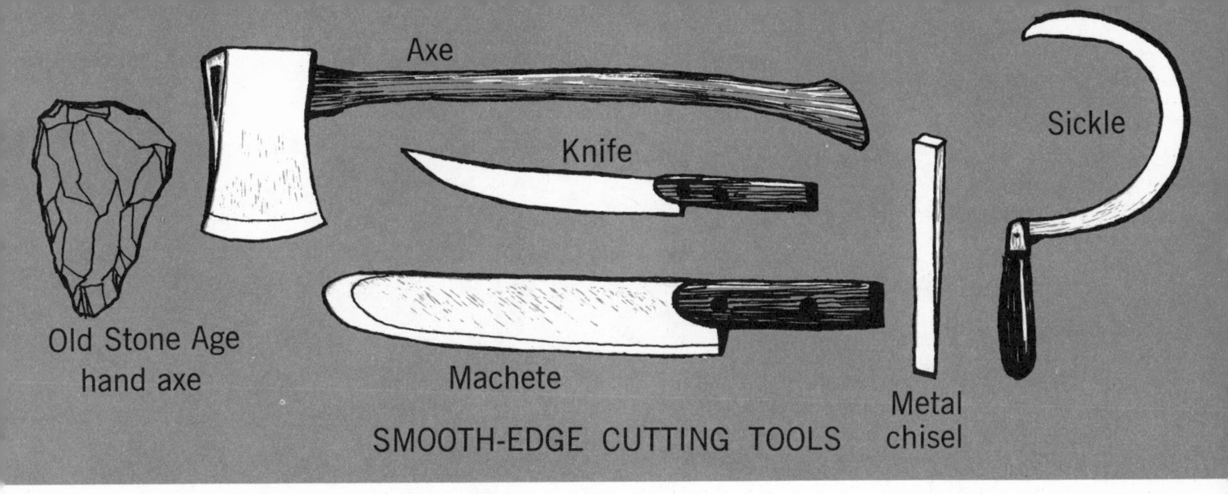

AXE: for splitting and chopping wood

KNIFE: for general cutting work

MACHETE: for clearing underbrush and for cutting sugar cane

SICKLE: for cutting grain and grass

METAL CHISEL: for splitting and cutting metals

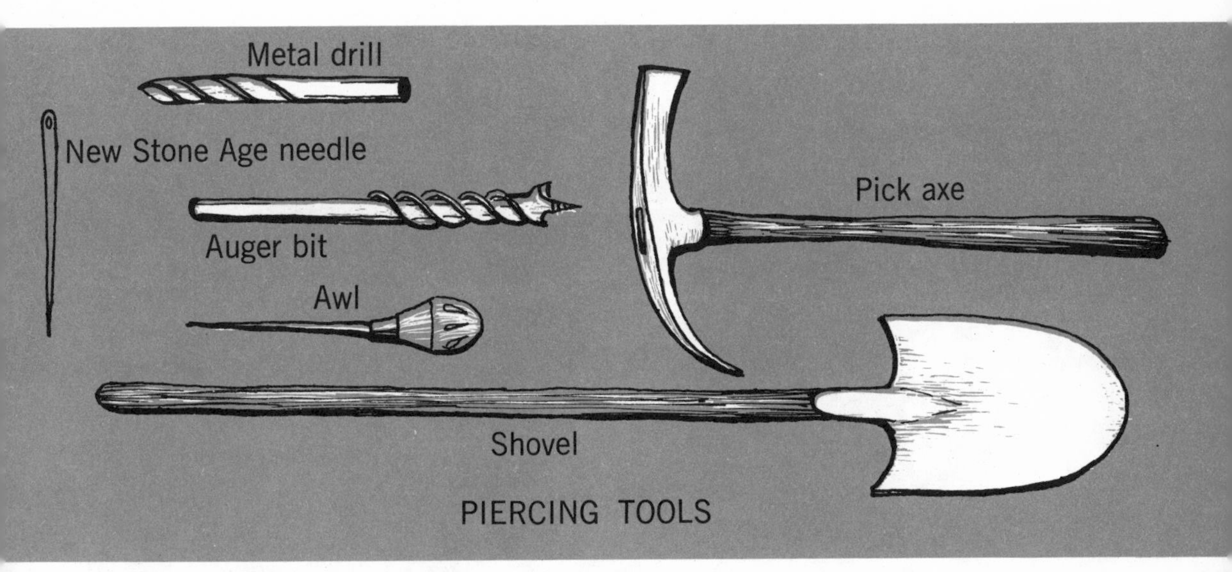

METAL DRILL: for making holes in metal

AUGER BIT: for making holes in wood

AWL: for making small holes

SHOVEL: for digging and carrying

PICK AXE: for splitting materials, such as coal and stone

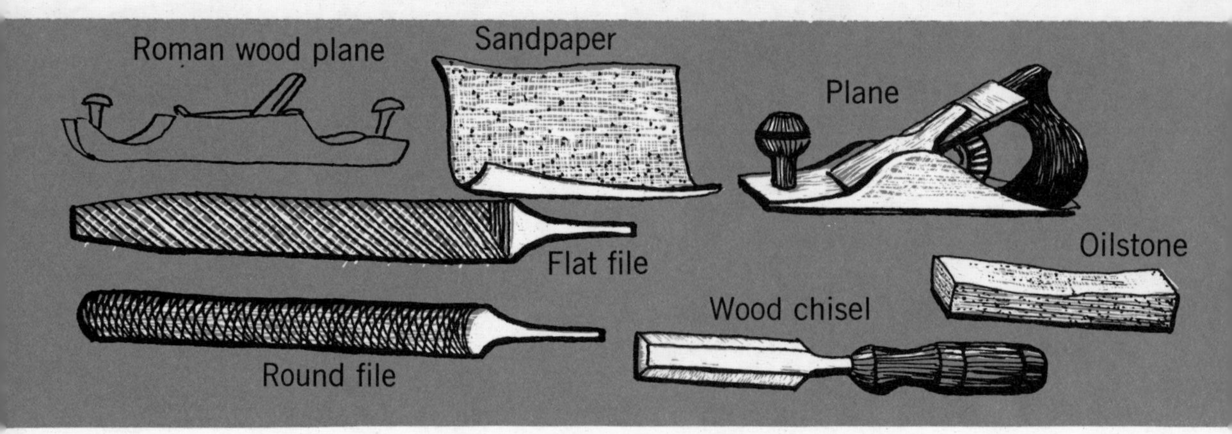

SURFACE SCRAPING TOOLS

FILES: for shaping and smoothing wood, metals, and plastics
SANDPAPER: for smoothing rough surfaces
PLANE: for paring wood to make it smooth and even
OILSTONE: for sharpening steel cutting edges
WOOD CHISEL: for cutting and gouging wood into various shapes

SHEARING TOOLS

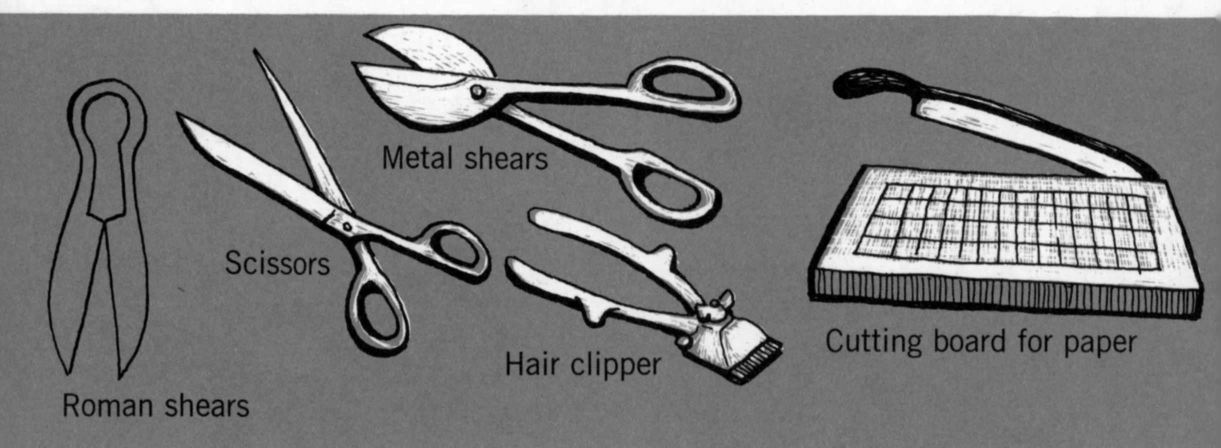

SHEARING TOOLS: two edges work against each other to cut material that is placed between them

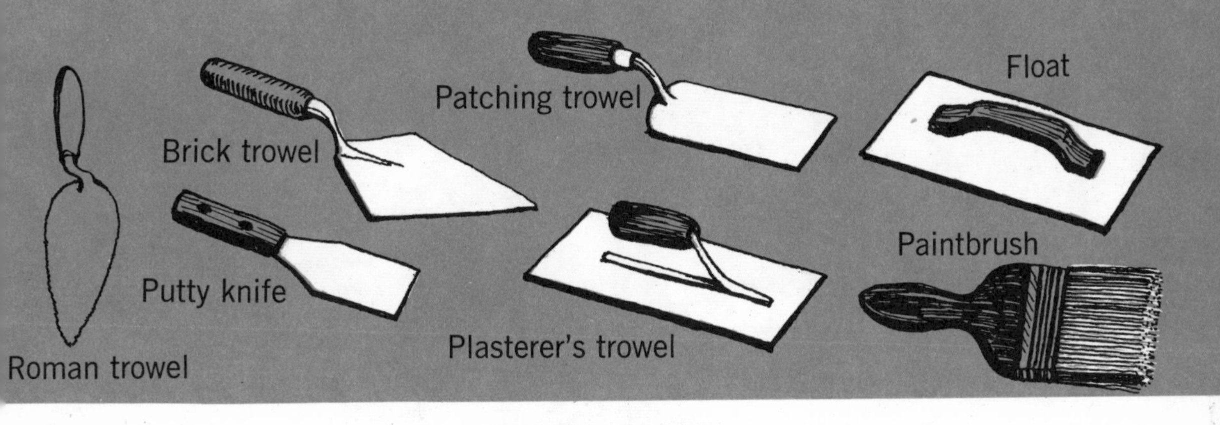

COVERING TOOLS

COVERING TOOLS: used to apply plaster, cement, putty, and paint, for protecting and decorating surfaces

JOINING TOOLS

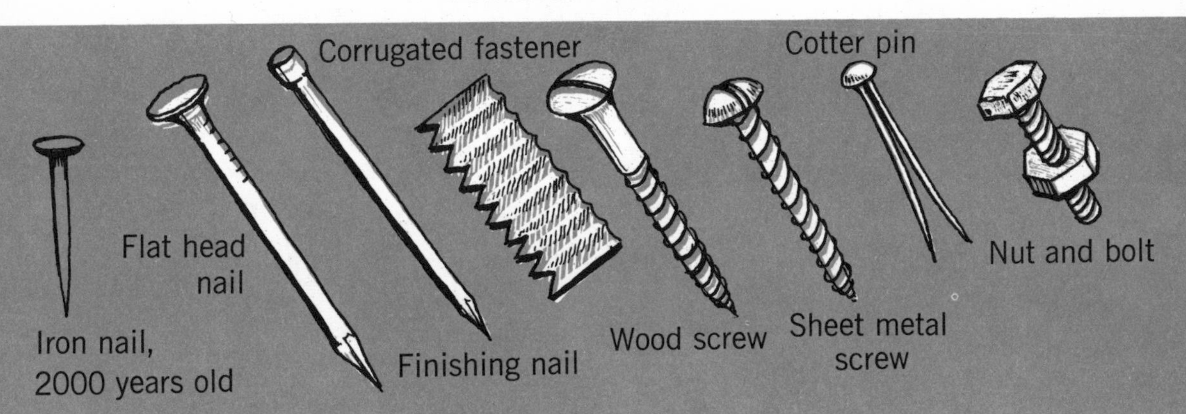

FLAT HEAD NAIL: for joining pieces of wood in rough work

FINISHING NAIL: for joining pieces of wood in fine work. The head of the nail is driven into the wood so that it does not show

CORRUGATED FASTENER: for joining the ends of two pieces of wood, as in a picture frame corner

WOOD SCREW: for fastening wood to hardware, different materials, or other pieces of wood

SHEET METAL SCREW: for fastening two pieces of thin metal

COTTER PIN: for loosely joining two parts, one of which is movable, as in the wheel and axle of an automobile

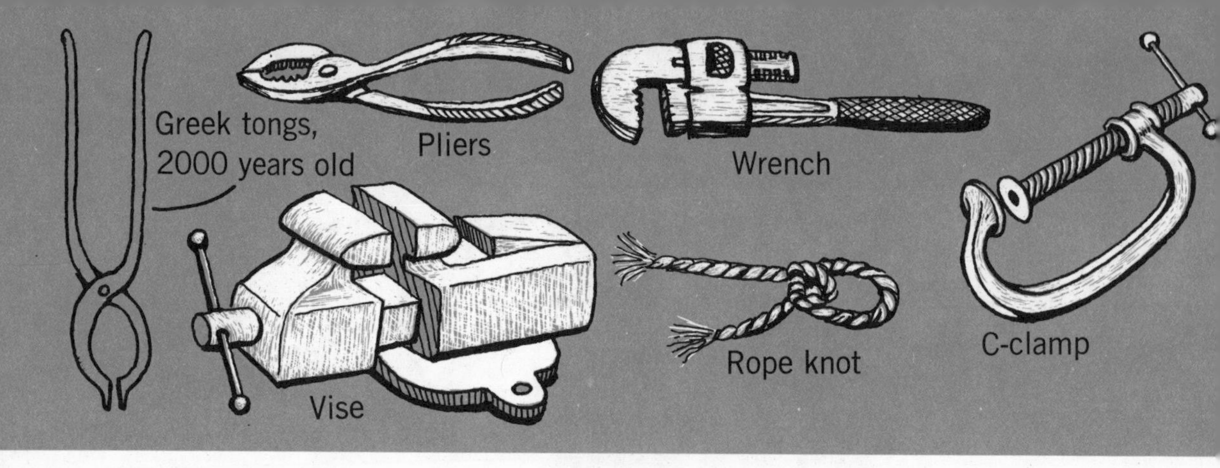

GRIPPING TOOLS

PLIERS: for gripping and holding small objects
VISE: for holding an object firmly so that it can be worked on
WRENCH: for gripping an object in order to twist it
ROPE KNOT: for fastening objects so that they do not move
C-CLAMP: for holding objects temporarily, as when they are being glued together

PULLEY: for lifting heavy objects, such as pianos and safes
JACKSCREW: for raising heavy objects — for example, an automobile with a flat tire
CROWBAR: for moving or raising weights a short distance

MOVING AND LIFTING TOOLS

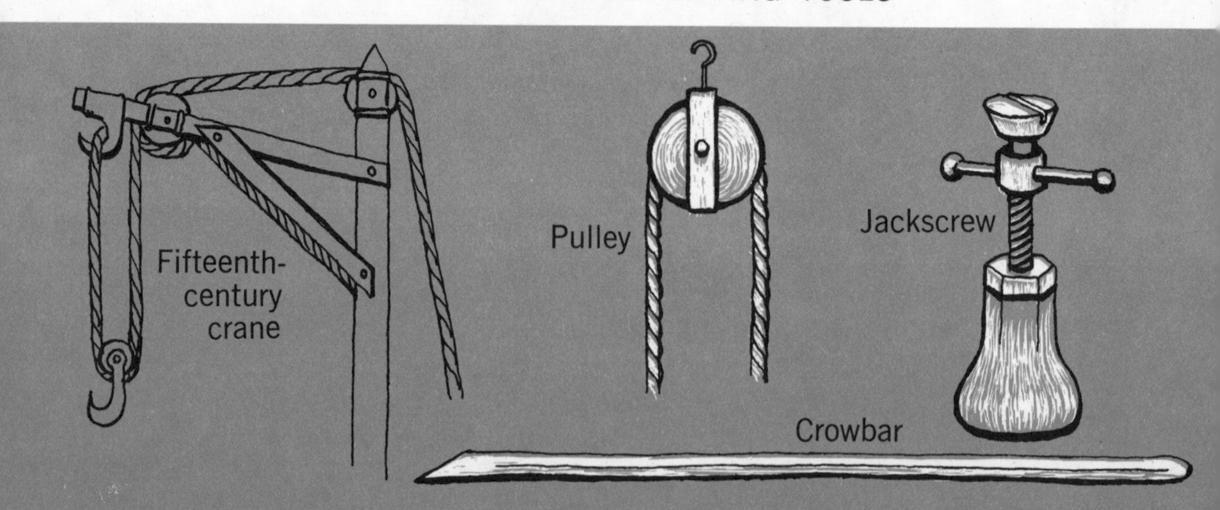

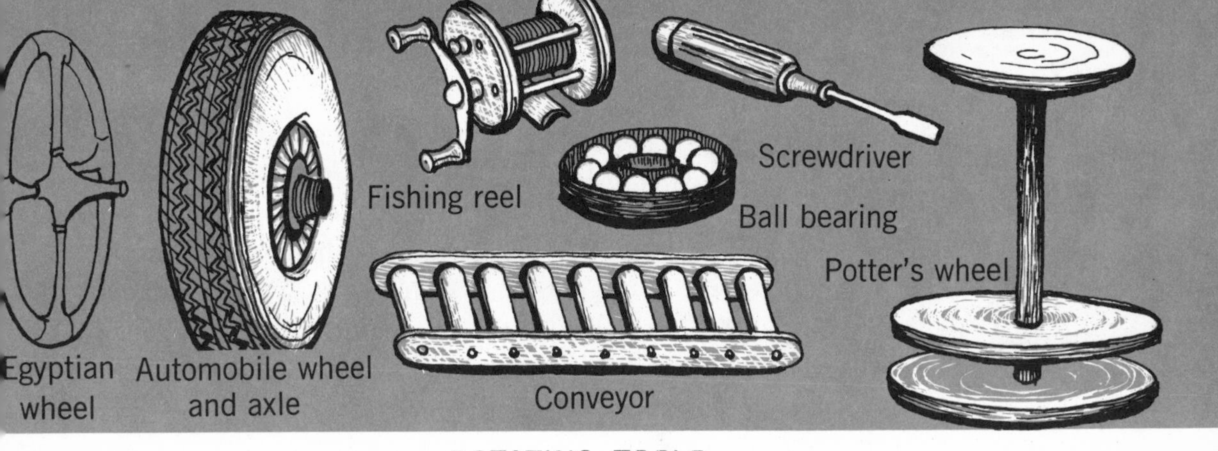

ROTATING TOOLS

AUTOMOBILE WHEEL: for changing motion sent from the engine into rolling motion

FISHING REEL: for unwinding and winding fishing line

BALL BEARING: for reducing friction so that a part can turn easily

SCREWDRIVER: for turning screws, generally to fasten or tighten objects

CONVEYOR: for moving objects from one place to another

POTTER'S WHEEL: for forming clay into rounded shapes, such as bowls and vases

GATHERING TOOLS: used to lengthen our reach and allow us to collect conveniently things which we cannot easily reach

GATHERING TOOLS

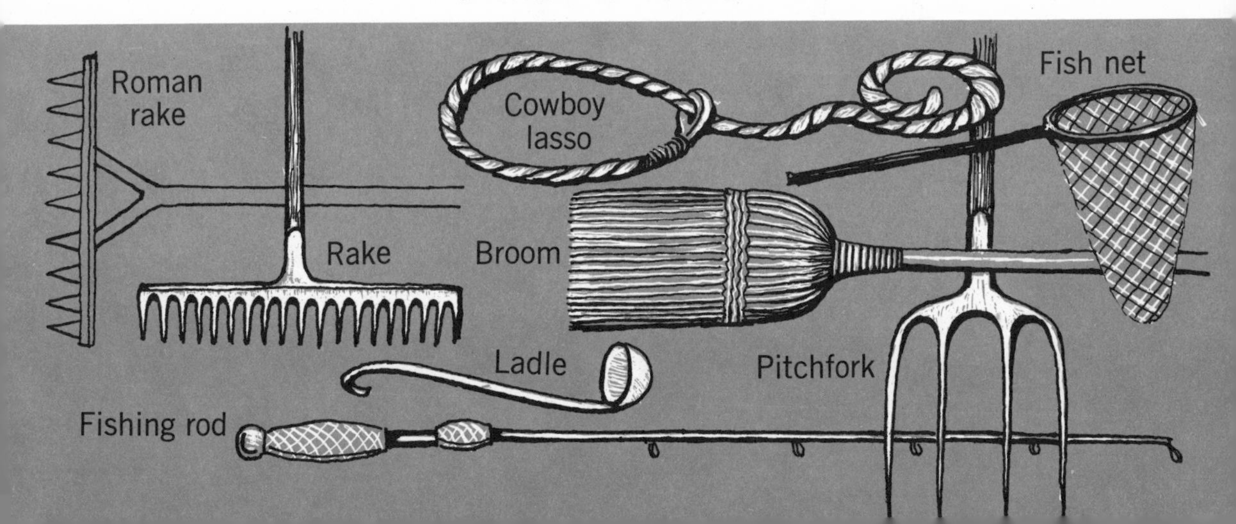

there has been no change in the total number of groups. The same 12 groups that we recognize today existed in ancient times.

Many tools that are in daily use in modern homes and shops were common 2000 years ago in Roman times; 3200 years ago, at the beginning of the Iron Age; 5000 years ago in the Bronze Age; and, with some exceptions, 7000 years ago in the New Stone Age.

Six Simple Machines

"GIVE me a place to stand and I will move the earth." So said Archimedes, the brilliant scientist and inventor, who lived in Greece over two thousand years ago. He was poetically describing the ability of a lever to move huge objects.

The lever is one of the six *simple machines*. The others are the pulley, the wheel and axle, the inclined plane, the wedge, and the screw. If you take apart any piece of complicated machinery, you will find that it is made up of some combination of these six simple machines.

Simple machines are devices which make work easier. With a lever a man can move a rock that weighs a great deal more than he does. Using pulleys he can raise a heavy steel safe to a high office window. If he has a flat tire, he can place a screw jack under an automobile that may weigh 3000 pounds or more and lift it easily.

Is It Work or Wasted Effort?

THE WORK that we do, whether we use a machine or our bare hands, is commonly measured in scientific units called foot-pounds. To a scientist the word *work* does not have the same meaning that it generally does in everyday life. If you push against a heavy bed and cannot move it, you have not done any work. You may feel tired because of the force you exerted, but in a scientific sense no work was accomplished. Should you try again and succeed in moving the bed, you will have performed work. In science, work is done only when a force successfully moves an object. By *force* we mean any push or pull that is exerted.

The amount of work done can be found by multiplying the force by the distance that the object has moved.

Example 1.

A lumberjack exerted a force of 45 pounds to drag a log 60 feet to the river's edge. How much work did he do? WORK = FORCE x DISTANCE. Therefore, WORK = 45 pounds (THE FORCE) x 60 feet (THE DISTANCE), or 45 pounds x 60 feet = 2700 foot-pounds.

One great benefit of machines is that they often enable a small force to overcome a large load.

Mechanical advantage is a numerical relationship that tells us how much actual help we may expect from a machine. To find the mechanical advantage of any machine, divide the load that the machine moves by the force applied to move the load, that is:

MECHANICAL ADVANTAGE = LOAD ÷ FORCE

Example 2.

A furniture mover, using a set of pulleys, exerted 50 pounds of force to lift a 200 pound crate. What is the mechanical advantage of the pulleys? MECHANICAL ADVANTAGE = LOAD ÷ FORCE. Therefore, MECHANICAL ADVANTAGE = 200 pounds (THE LOAD) ÷ 50 pounds (THE FORCE), or 200 pounds ÷ 50 pounds = 4.

The mechanical advantage of 4 means that for every pound of force applied by the man, 4 pounds of load were lifted by the pulleys. Since the man applied 50 pounds of force, a total load of 50 pounds x 4, or 200 pounds, was lifted.

Pulleys

PULLEYS are weight-lifting machines that can be used singly or in combinations. Another way to find the mechanical advantage of a pulley system is to add up the number of ropes that support the load that is being lifted. Figure 1 shows you how to do this.

Example 3.

Using pulley system D, which has a mechanical advantage of 4, a man must exert 50 pounds of force to raise a 200 pound load, since 4 x 50 = 200. The mechanical advantage also reveals the distance the rope travels. For every foot that the weight is raised, the rope must be pulled out 4 feet.

FIGURE 1: PULLEY SYSTEMS

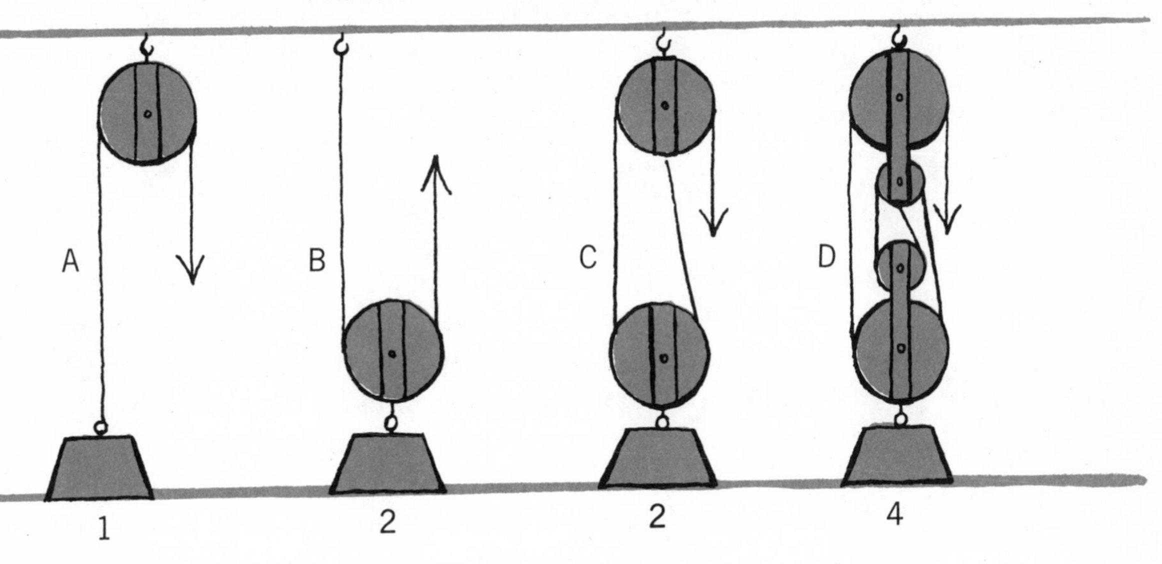

The mechanical advantage equals the number of ropes supporting the load — shown by the numbers in the diagram

If the load were raised 10 feet, how far would the rope be pulled out? The rope would be pulled out 40 feet, since 4 x 10 = 40.

In this same Example, how much *work* does the man do to raise the load 10 feet? WORK = FORCE X DISTANCE. Therefore, WORK = 50 pounds (THE FORCE) x 40 feet (THE DISTANCE), or 50 pounds x 40 feet = 2000 foot-pounds.

How much work does the pulley system itself do? WORK = FORCE X DISTANCE. Therefore, WORK = 200 POUNDS (THE FORCE, OR LOAD) x 10 feet (THE DISTANCE), or 200 pounds x 10 feet = 2000 foot-pounds.

Thus the work of the man, equals the work of the pulley system.

The Law of Work

A MACHINE cannot do more work than is put into it. This is one of the great laws of nature. It is called the *law of work*.

Friction Uses up Force

WHEN a pulley system is in use, the rope constantly drags against the wheel. Some of the force that is exerted on the pulley system is wasted because it has to overcome this dragging, or *friction*. Otherwise the rope and wheel would not move. This wasted force, or *effort*, reduces the actual work that the pulley system performs.

In any machine, all of the force that is applied is never completely changed into work. A part of it is always lost to friction. However, it is easier to understand what machines do and how they operate if we *neglect* the drag of friction. Frequently scientists and engineers find it helpful to pretend that such frictionless machines exist. They are called *ideal machines*.

The work that goes into an ideal machine exactly equals the work that it produces. Another way of saying this is that in an ideal machine WORK INPUT = WORK OUTPUT. Is the pulley system in example 3 an ideal machine?

The Lever

THE LEVER is perhaps the best known of the simple machines. A crowbar, a seesaw, a fishing pole, and the human arm itself are familiar levers. They are, in the language of science, bars that turn on a point. The point is called the *fulcrum*. Some simple machines,

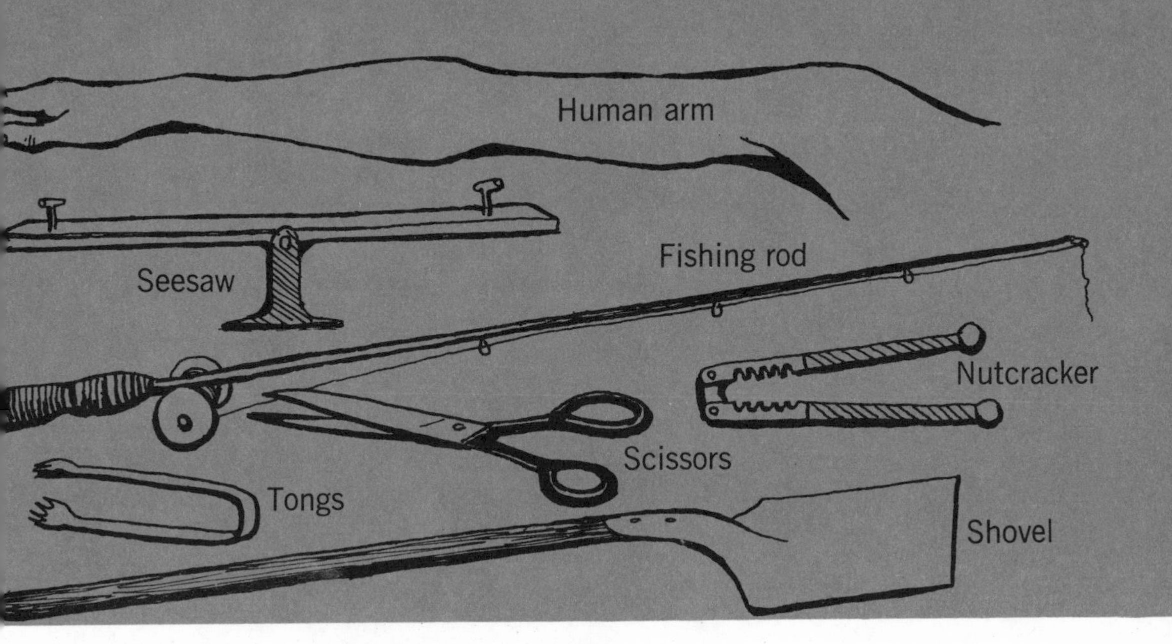

EVERYDAY LEVERS

like scissors, tweezers, and tongs are really two levers that share the same fulcrum.

All levers have a fulcrum on which to turn, a place where the force is applied, and a place where the load resists the force. The locations of the fulcrum, the force, and the load decide the *class* of a lever. There are three classes of levers, all shown in Figure 2.

FIGURE 2: THE THREE TYPES OF LEVERS

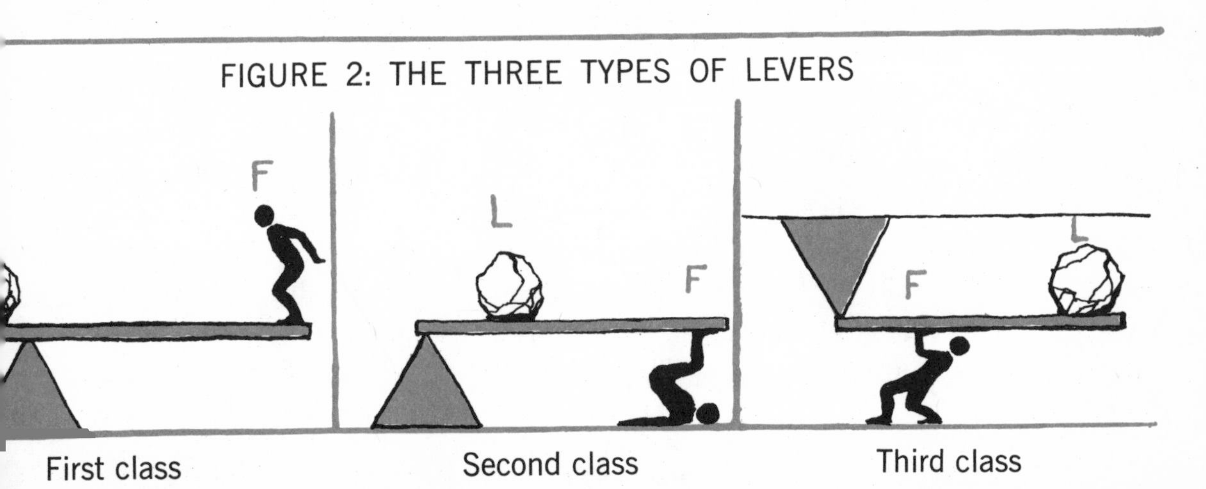

FIGURE 3: A FIRST CLASS LEVER IN USE

Example 4.

The force arm in Figure 3 is 4 feet long, and the load arm is 1 foot long. What is the mechanical advantage of the lever?

MECHANICAL ADVANTAGE = LOAD ARM ÷ FORCE ARM. Therefore, MECHANICAL ADVANTAGE = 4 feet (THE FORCE ARM) ÷ 1 foot (THE LOAD ARM), or 4 feet ÷ 1 foot = 4.

If the rock weighs 240 pounds, how many pounds of force must the man use to lift it?

The mechanical advantage equals 4, so that for every 4 pounds of load, the man must exert 1 pound of force. To lift the 240 pound rock, he has to push down with a force of 240 ÷ 4 = 60 pounds.

The lever is pushed down 12 inches. How high is the rock raised?

With a mechanical advantage of 4, the rock will rise 1 inch for every 4 inches that the man pushes down. When he pushes down 12 inches, the rock will be raised 12 ÷ 4 = 3 inches off the ground.

The Wheel and Axle

WHEN you turn a doorknob, you are using a simple machine called the *wheel and axle*. The knob is the wheel and the shaft that is hidden in the door is the axle. A light force on the knob turns the shaft, which pulls the latch back and opens the door. Other examples of the wheel and axle are a pencil sharpener, the windlass

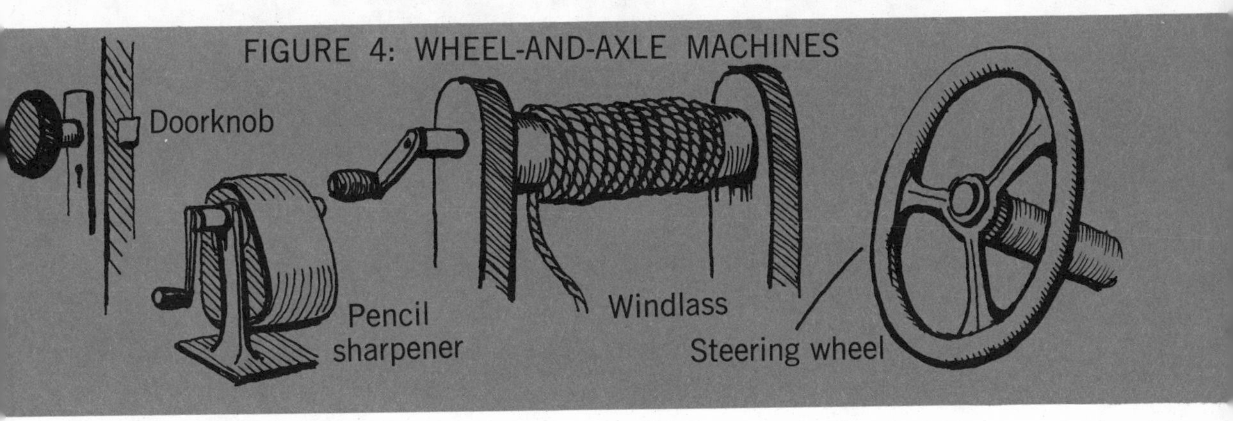

shown in Figure 4, the capstan for raising a ship's anchor, and the steering wheel of an automobile.

In wheel and axle machines, the wheel is rigidly fixed to the shaft and both turn together. The mechanical advantage of the wheel and axle is found by dividing the diameter of the wheel by the diameter of the axle.

The Inclined Plane

INCLINED planes are used to raise heavy loads to a higher level. Figure 5 shows four men lifting a barrel onto a platform. One

FIGURE 5: ONE MAN DOES THE WORK OF FOUR

man could do the job as well if he rolled the barrel up an inclined plane that had a mechanical advantage of 4. The mechanical advantage of an inclined plane equals the length of the plane divided by its height at the raised end.

Some inclined planes that make work easier are ramps, like the one used on the truck in Figure 5, stairways, ship gangplanks, and roads that go uphill.

Example 5.

What is the mechanical advantage of the truck ramp in Figure 5?

MECHANICAL ADVANTAGE = LENGTH ÷ HEIGHT. Therefore, MECHANICAL ADVANTAGE = 12 feet (THE LENGTH) ÷ 3 feet (THE HEIGHT), or 12 feet ÷ 3 feet = 4.

Could one man pushing with a force of 30 pounds roll a 100 pound barrel up the ramp?

Yes, because the mechanical advantage of 4 means that the man will use 1 pound of force for every 4 pounds of the load. Since he is using 30 pounds of force, the load that he can push is 30 x 4 = 120 pounds. The barrel only weighs 100 pounds, and a pushing force of 120 pounds will do the job easily.

The Wedge

FIGURE 6 shows that the wedge is really a combination of two inclined planes. Knives, axes, chisels, and nails are examples of common wedges. Most wedges are used to penetrate an object and split, cut, or make holes in it. A wedge that is thin and long has a higher mechanical advantage than one that is thick and short. For this reason a thin nail is easier to drive into wood than a thick nail. Wedges are also frequently used to raise very heavy objects short distances off the floor, as in Figure 6.

FIGURE 6: WEDGES ARE DOUBLE INCLINED PLANES

The Screw

THE SCREW is a special form of the inclined plane. If the thread of a screw were unwound, it would look like a spiral stairway – or a curved inclined plane. The wood screw, the cork screw, the nut and bolt, the vise, and the jackscrew are widely used examples of this powerful machine. The jackscrew is a large screw that fits into a solid base. It is turned by a handle that fits into the top of the screw. Because a jackscrew has a very high mechanical advantage, it is used to lift heavy weights, like an automobile, or the side of a house.

THE SCREW EXERTS GREAT FORCE

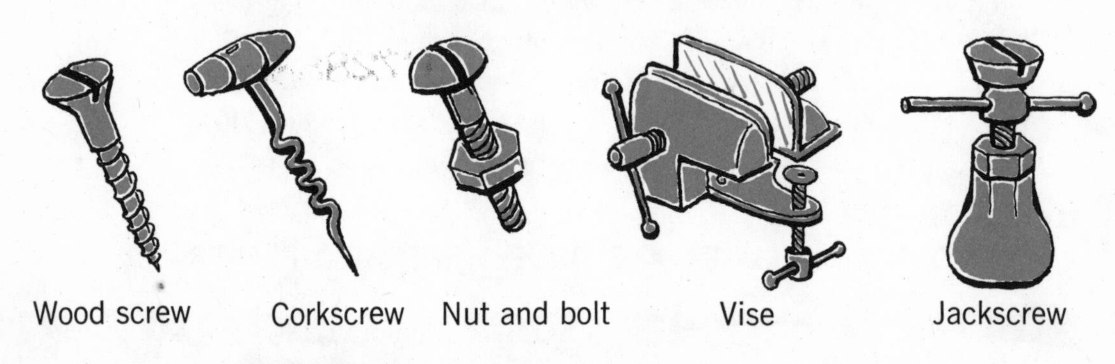

The Wheel and Other Moving Circles

AMONG man's most prized inventions are two tools that operate by moving in circles. One is the familiar wheel of transportation, and the other is the less familiar wheel of the potter. Both are about 5500 years old.

The importance of wheels to wagons, trains, automobiles, planes,

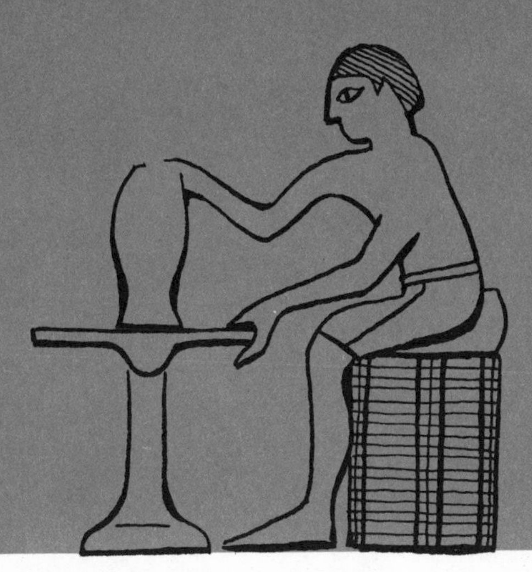

Almost 5000 years ago an Egyptian craftsman shaped this tall vase on a potter's wheel

Italian potters of the sixteenth century produced pottery by rotating a kick wheel with their feet

and many machines and devices is easily recognized. The contribution of the *potter's wheel,* however, is often overlooked.

In early times pottery allowed both the farmer and the city dweller to cook foods and store what was left over. Cooking in pottery also added many foods which could be boiled or stewed, but not baked or roasted. Because of farming and pottery, the daily needs of eating became less dependent on accidents and luck. The pottery supply of primitive people was as necessary to their way of life as modern pots, pans, glasses, and storage containers are to our own.

The potter's wheel was a flat disk that rotated on a central pivot. A lump of clay was placed in the middle of the disk. Then while the disk was kept spinning rapidly, the potter shaped the clay with his hands. He produced round pots and jars in minutes instead of the hours that it formerly took to mold them by hand.

The ancestor of the rolling wheel was a log that was pushed and rolled along the ground. Such log-wheels were clumsy, however, and could be used only for very crude transportation. They were improved by making a solid wheel out of three pieces of wood fastened together by cross bars.

After people learned to mount one or two pairs of the solid wheels beneath platforms, the first wagons started to roll. These wagons were powered by oxen and by *onagers,* animals that resembled horses. The onagers died off some 4000 years ago and were replaced by horses.

The earliest wagons were used to transport farm produce to villages, as funeral cars for royalty, and as troop transports for carrying soldiers to battlefields. After lighter wagons developed, such as the war chariots used in combat, the solid wheel gradually disappeared. It was too cumbersome where speed and the ability to turn quickly were required.

A spoked wheel took its place. This new, lighter wheel was made with a separate rim for the outside, a separate hub for the center, and bars, or spokes, to connect the two. These three inventions — the rim, the hub, and the spokes — are still the most important parts of wheels made today.

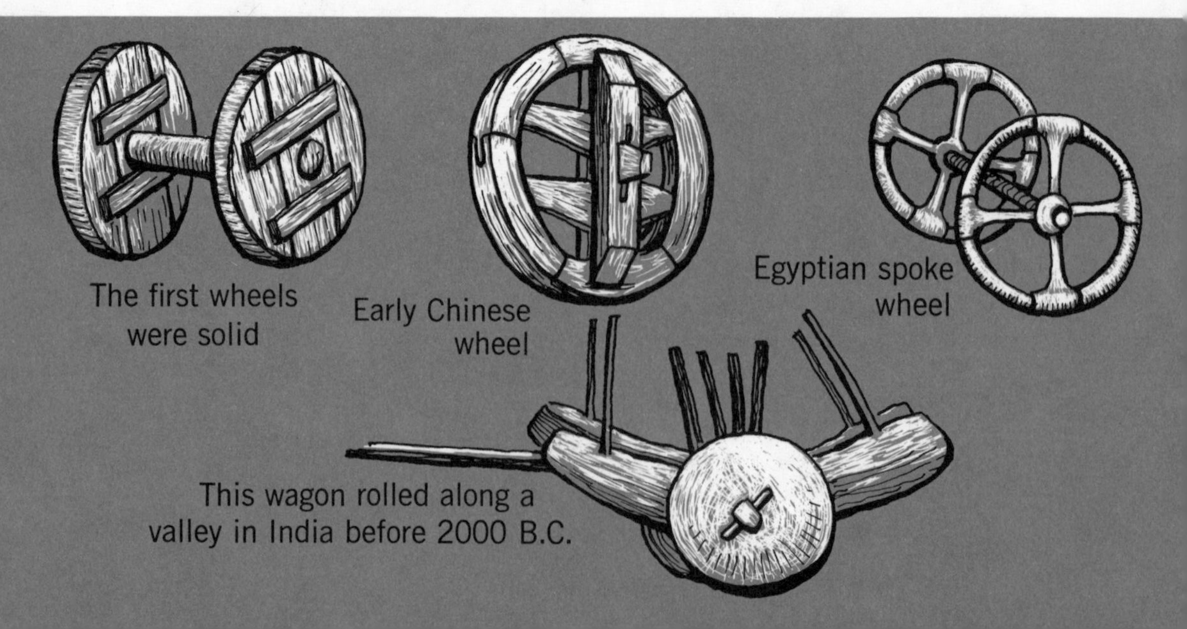

The illustrations in this section show how other tools that move in a circle will drill holes, make fire, grind flour, and spin thread. These tools have not completely disappeared. They continue to be made and used in some primitive regions where life today seems still a part of the Stone Ages.

The Discovery of Tools

How were man's basic group of 12 tools invented? And what was man's first tool?

We can only guess at the answers to these questions, for there are no records that go back that far into the past. But after man started to use tools and later to make them, we know that he began to be different from the animals.

It was probably in their never-ending search for food that the men of the Old Stone Age made the great discovery of tools. Lying on the ground around them were rocks, branches, and occasionally shells and the long bones of dead animals. Some men picked up these crude objects and found that they could be used for gathering and hunting food. Digging with a broken branch for roots in the ground seems simple enough to us today. But for these primitive people it was an act of glorious imagination. It meant that in their minds they could see that a tool would do better work than just a bare hand. This vision would forever change the way men lived.

One day a hammer would allow them to pound harder and with greater force than they could with bare fists. A shovel would scoop up earth faster than fingers. A spear would lengthen the distance they could extend their arms. A knife would cut faster and better than teeth and hands. A lever would move weights that their bodies could not budge. These and many other tools would give men the strength and reach to grow in their environment.

A Prehistoric Story

In the last light of early evening, the Valley Man is digging in the ground for roots to eat. It is early spring, one million years ago, and the Valley Man's fingers hurt because the ground is still hard with the freeze of winter. When he pauses to rest his fingers, he notices a small branch beside him. The branch has no value for it cannot be eaten. After widening the hole, the Valley man again stops to quiet the ache in his fingers. The branch is still there and he looks at it once more. It is about as thick as his fingers. If it could only do their work!

Still using his fingers, he starts to make the hole deeper. In a little while the rhythm of his digging gets slower, skips a few beats, and then stops. The Valley Man cannot forget the thought of the branch doing the work of his fingers.

Picking up the branch, he clumsily pushes it into the ground.

As he pulls it out, a small amount of dirt is removed. Again he pushes the branch in and scoops out more dirt. The Valley Man continues to dig. His excitement increases as he learns that the hard, pointed branch penetrates the ground better than his fingers. A glimpse of a rounded, yellow surface and he begins to work faster. Soon the root is uncovered and eaten. When he leaves, the Valley Man takes the branch with him, holding it in fingers that no longer hurt.

His new tool is the ancestor of the digging stick, the pickaxe, the spade, the hand shovel, and the giant steam shovel.

Stone, Wood, and Bone

THE MEN of the Old Stone Age gradually learned to rely on tools for work and for hunting. At first they did not try to change the objects they picked up from the ground. These were used in the natural forms in which they were found.

In later years men slowly developed from simple users of tools

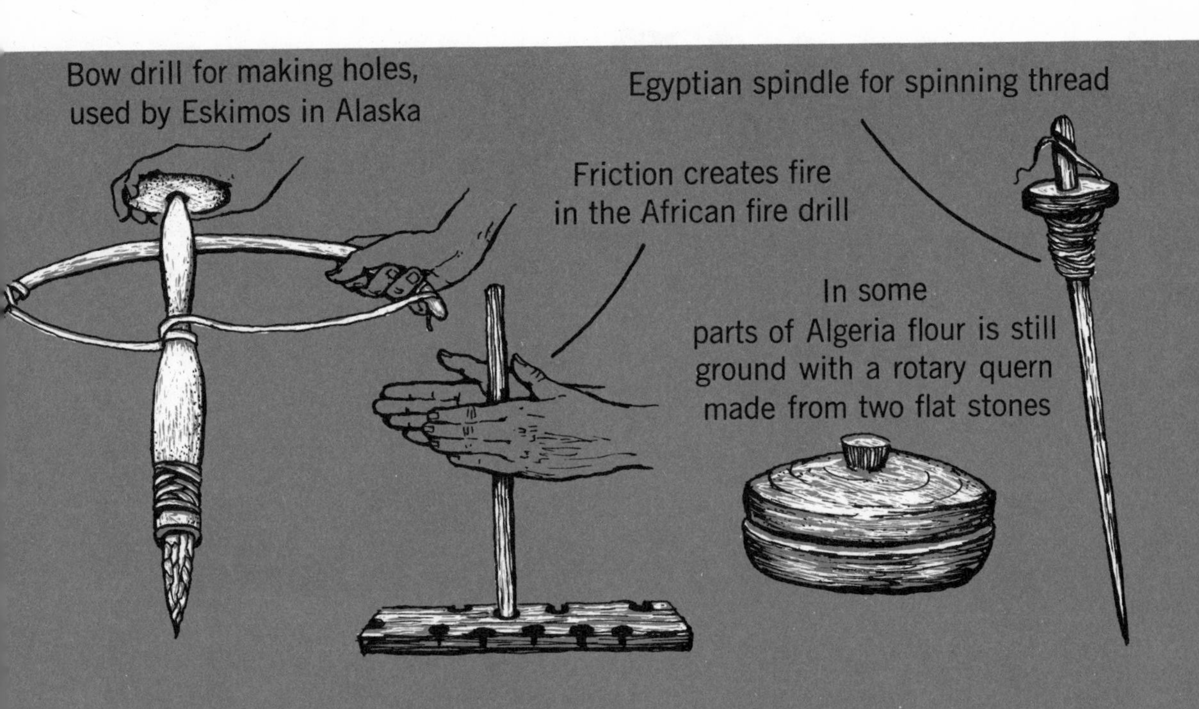

into makers of tools. They learned that a digging stick penetrates deeper if the point is sharpened. A hand axe has a better grip if its top is wrapped in animal skin. A pole for knocking down fruit is easier to wield if the side branches are stripped from the main branch. A blunt stone can be shattered into sharp splinters and cutting edges if it is hit with another stone.

As toolmaking progressed, men mastered the use of different materials, such as stone, wood, bone, antler, ivory, and shell. These materials were frequently difficult to work with. Patience and great skill were necessary to finish even a single tool.

Flint was the most popular of all the stones that the primitive toolmaker used. When flint is hammered with another stone, it can be chipped into a desired shape. It is a hard and brittle substance that fractures easily. An experienced flint craftsman could produce cutting tools with edges that were almost razor sharp.

In the Old Stone Age flint was found on cliffs and along rivers

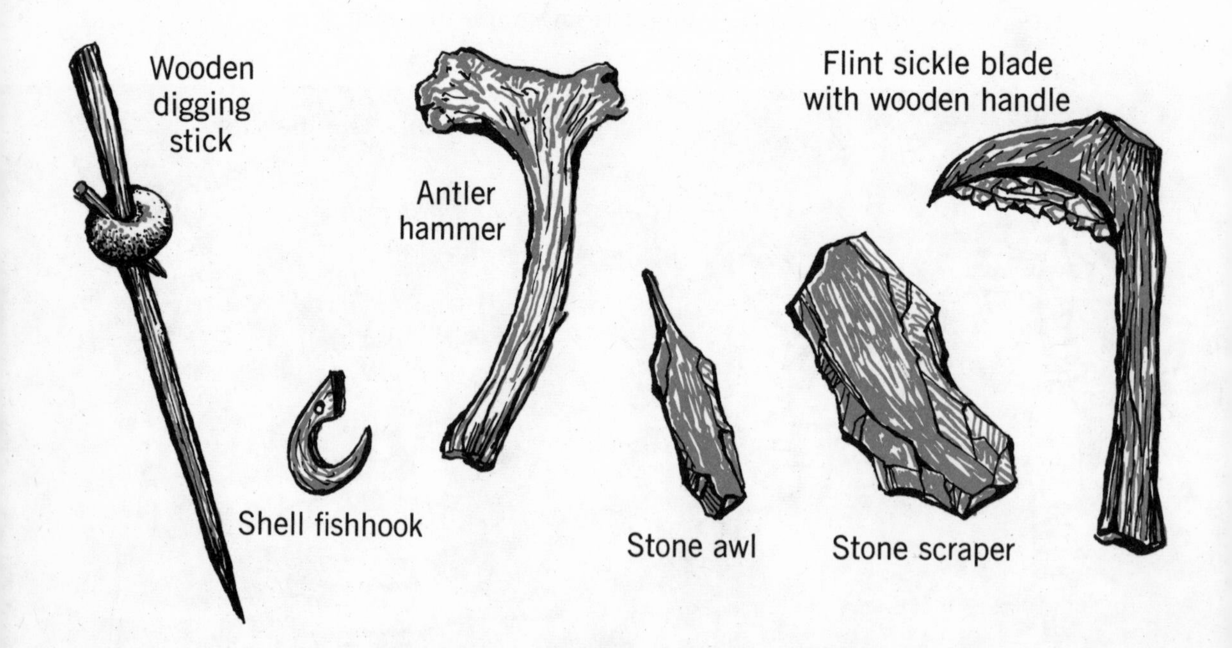

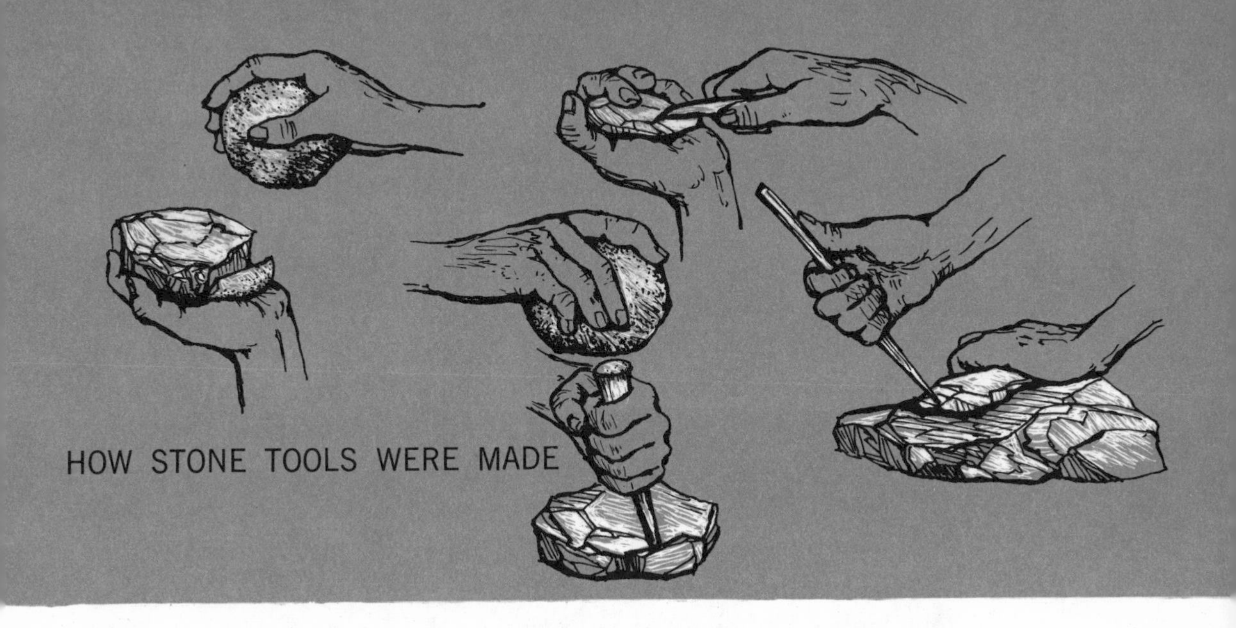

and beaches. Hundreds of thousands of years later, the men of the New Stone Age learned to operate crude flint mines. They followed ridges of flint deep into the ground, working with picks made of deer antlers and shovels made of the bones of oxen.

Other stones, like *obsidian* and *chert,* were also important in toolmaking. Black and glossy obsidian is a natural glass formed from volcanic lava. Chert is very similar to flint but it has a rougher grain.

On a visit to a museum. you can see some of the tools of primitive man. With few exceptions, all of them will be made of stone. Stone is durable and is not easily destroyed. The name Old Stone Age was given to this early period because stone tools which were made at that time have survived and can be studied today. Almost all wooden tools have simply decayed and disappeared. Though bone, antler, ivory, and shell last longer than wood, tools made of these materials have mostly vanished too. Over the ages they have simply disintegrated into dust.

Wood, still one of our most valuable building materials, was of great value to the ancients. They used it to erect rough shelters and to make tools, such as digging sticks, clubs, and long poles. Much later wood, and occasionally bone, were used to construct handles and shafts.

Handles offer convenience and protection to the hands. They permit some tools, such as axes and hammers, to be raised high and brought down with great force. On hoes and rakes, handles provide a long reach that covers a wide area.

Shafts are used on spears and arrows to launch and direct their flight over long distances. Originally these missiles were made of one piece. Their ends were sharpened either by cutting with a stone knife or by charring with fire. As the design of weapons improved, separate tips of stone or bone were added.

Hammer heads, axe blades, and sharp points were lashed to handles and shafts with early forms of rope. To make rope, primitive man twisted grass, vegetable fibers, hair, and strips of hide together, building them up to the desired thicknesses and lengths. With this simple spinning method, he also produced rope for fishing lines, fishing nets and snares, and land nets to catch animals.

Ages after the first strands were twisted, rope was used by a race of men called Cro-Magnon for the unusual purpose of stringing ornamental necklaces. Some of the pictures and carvings that dec-

One of the oldest wooden tools ever found, this piece of a spear is 250,000 years old

Present-day Eskimos hunt fish with a double-pronged spear

orated Cro-Magnon caves and tools are still in existence. Today, 30,000 years after this art was created, we still find it bold and exciting to look at. The Cro-Magnons were guided by their sense of beauty when they shaped tools of flint, bone, antler, ivory, and shell. Their needles, harpoon heads, fishhooks, knives, axes, awls, and adzes reveal artistry and gifted workmanship.

Growing and Grinding

AS THE Old Stone Age gave way to the New Stone Age, great changes took place in the way men lived. This period, which began in different areas seven to eleven thousand years ago, was the early dawn of civilization.

In the New Stone Age men gradually learned to grow their own food instead of searching for it as did their ancestors. From wanderers, they became settled farmers. Men continued to hunt and fish, but they also raised animals for food and planted fruits and cereal grains, like barley, wheat, and rye. Their houses were permanent and well constructed, containing fireplaces, cooking areas, and sometimes even porches. A typical New Stone Age village might have 35 houses grouped in an area of less than one acre.

Meat was cooked by boiling and roasting. Cereal grains were eaten uncooked, mixed with hot water to make porridge or ground into flour for biscuits and bread.

Fires were started by striking a mineral called iron pyrites against a piece of flint. The hot flying sparks produced by the blows ignited dry wood chips. A modern cigarette lighter, with its steel wheel, stick of flint, and wick, practically duplicates this ancient method of making fire.

The farmers of the New Stone Age used simple tools to help

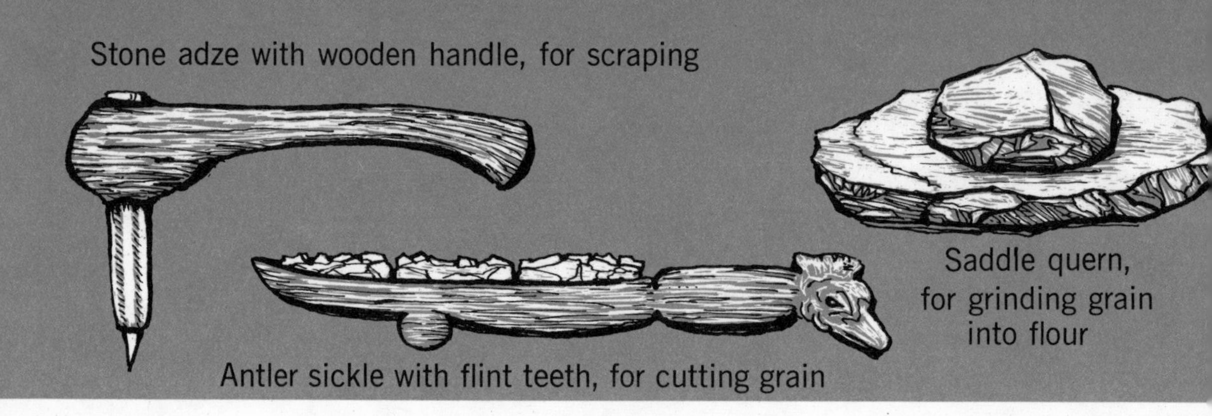

THREE TOOLS FROM THE NEW STONE AGE

them plant and harvest their grains. Before planting began, they broke up and loosened the soil with a digging stick. But the digging stick was not a satisfactory tool for working large areas of land. Later, in the New Stone Age, it was changed into a hoe by attaching a stone blade to its end. The new hoe was better than the digging stick for turning over soil, and it could be used to remove weeds. When the harvest came, the ripe cereal plant was cut with sickles made of sharp flint flakes set into handles of bone or wood. Frequently sickle handles were carved into the shape of animal heads.

The harvested cereal grain was usually divided into three portions: one to be stored and eaten during later months; another to be stored and planted for the next crop; and the third to be made into flour.

Flour is simply very finely-ground pieces of cereal grain. It was made by the men of the New Stone Age in two ways. In the first the grain was placed in a stone jug called a *mortar*, where it was ground and crushed with a stone hammer called a *pestle*. The mortar and pestle were invented by the cave dwellers of the Old Stone Age to grind pigments for their paintings. They are still used

BOWLS

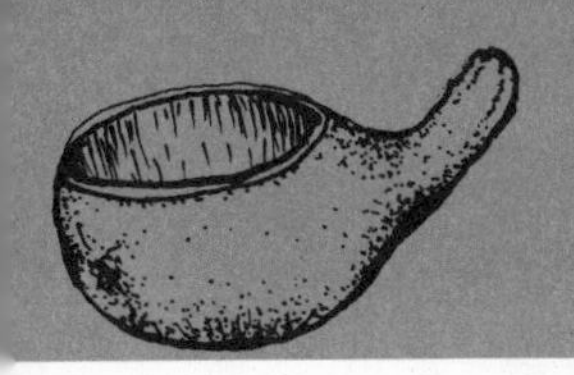
Gourd

Stone

Sea shell

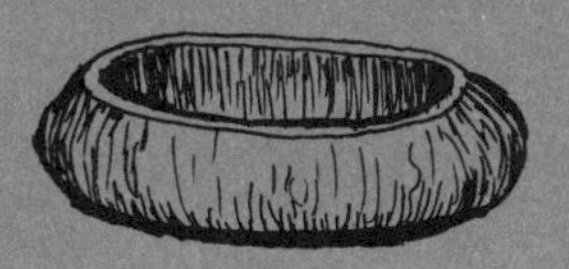
Wood

in laboratories and drugstores to grind chemicals that are large or lumpy. Grain was also ground into flour by placing it on a large flat stone and rubbing it with a smaller flat stone. This tool, which is made of two stones, is known as a *saddle quern.*

Although many improvements were made in their design, flat stones remained the principal tool for grinding flour for thousands of years. Variations of the ancient saddle quern were used until the end of the 19th century, when pairs of rollers replaced the giant stones of large flour mills.

"Inventions breed inventions," said Ralph Waldo Emerson. This was as true for the New Stone Age as it is for our own times. The invention of early farming methods gave men a new diet and new habits of eating. It also gave them some new problems. How could the food that was grown be cooked? Where could it be stored? The solutions to these problems were not found for many years.

At first the people of the New Stone Age tried to use the containers they already had. These were sea shells, bowls chipped out of stone and wood and gourds. (Gourds are fruits whose shells make handy containers.) The increasing surplus of flour and seeds, however, inspired the women to invent new ways of making storage baskets.

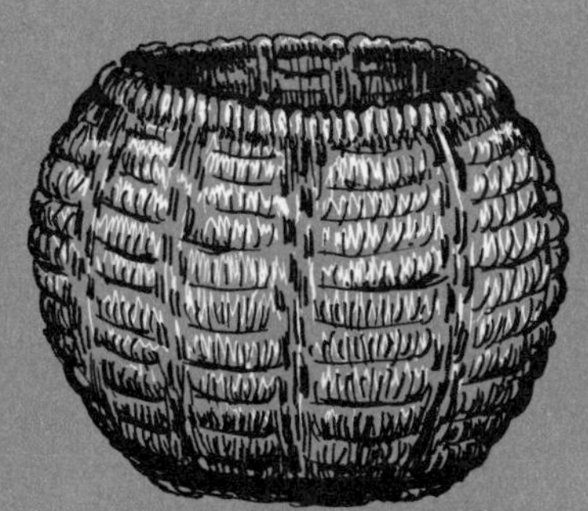
Egyptian basket preserved over 5000 years

Working with reeds, grass, and straw, they developed basket weaving techniques that are still known and widely used throughout the modern world. An unusual example of how baskets have not changed much since the New Stone Age can be found in the Egyptian town of El Fayum. Here weavers continue to copy the style of baskets that were first made around 5000 B.C.

Basketmaking also taught the imaginative farm people of the New Stone Age how to weave. Ropemaking, which had been invented by their ancestors, led to spinning and weaving, and the making of cloth.

To spin thread, fibers were pulled out from plants, such as flax, and twisted together. Skilled spinners were able to form these fibers into strong threads of suitable lengths and thicknesses. The threads were woven into cloth on an early loom that was just a simple frame. A set of parallel threads, called the *warp,* was attached lengthwise one next to the other, to two opposite sides of the loom. The long *weft* thread was then passed over and under each warp

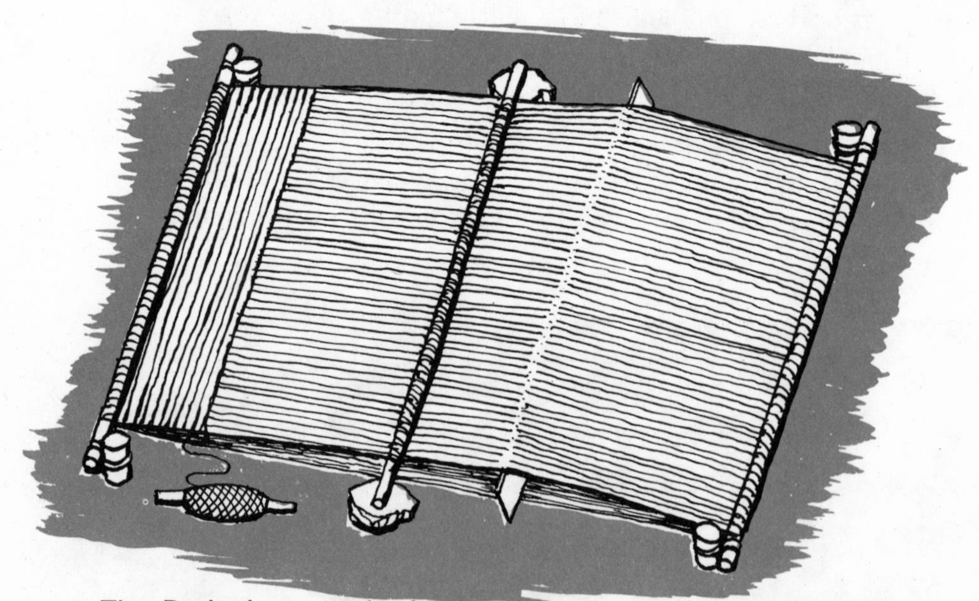

The Bedouin nomads, in the Near East, still weave cloth on a 5000-year-old invention—the ancient Egyptian horizontal ground loom

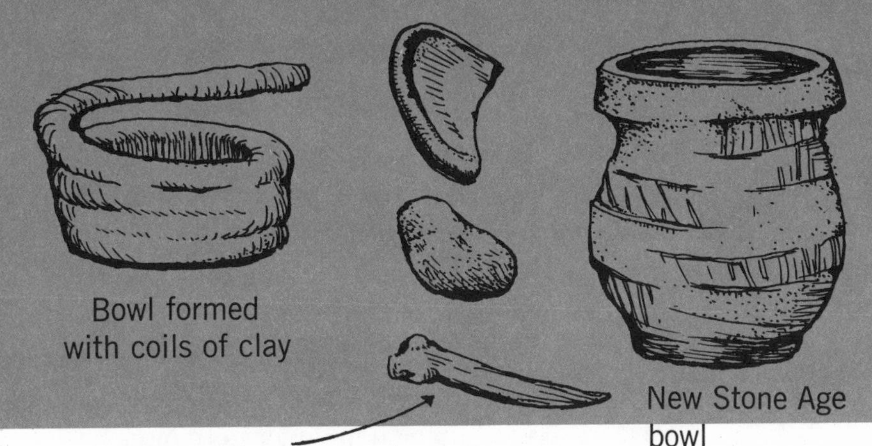

thread. Back and forth across the loom went the weft thread until all the spaces were filled and the cloth was finished.

If a woman who lived at the beginning of the New Stone Age were asked what her kitchen lacked, she might have replied, "Some containers that will hold liquids and not be damaged by heating." As farming improved, the need for better cooking equipment increased. Kitchens became the birthplace of pottery.

The word *pottery* describes any object, from a button to a bowl, that is molded out of clay and then hardened by fire. The heat from the fire solidifies the clay by changing it chemically and driving off water.

After potters formed the clay to a desired shape of, say, a bowl or jar, they partially dried their work in the sun. Then they baked it in the intense heat of a very hot fire. Starting with a soft mass of clay, potters were able to produce permanent shapes that resisted heat and were hard as stone.

Grinding is another process that was given to us by the inventive minds of the New Stone Age. The farmers of this period observed that after two rocks were rubbed together, their surfaces became worn and smooth. When a rock like *schist* was used for the rubbing, the edge of a stone-cutting tool could be ground to an unusual sharpness. Ground edges took a long time to make, but they were tough and cut far better than edges made by the earlier process of chipping. Working with axes that had ground edges, farmers were able to chop down trees more easily and increase the size of their farms.

Tools that were ground, like the axe, adze, knife, and chisel, also advanced woodworking skills. Fine cabinet makers today still use the *mortise and tenon,* a special joint invented by the farmer-craftsmen of the New Stone Age for connecting two pieces of wood. These early carpenters used wood to build new and improved houses, benches, canoes, and ladles and bowls. In many ways the cutting edges that they ground on stone carpentry tools resemble the edges on modern steel tools.

Mortise and tenon joint for connecting wood

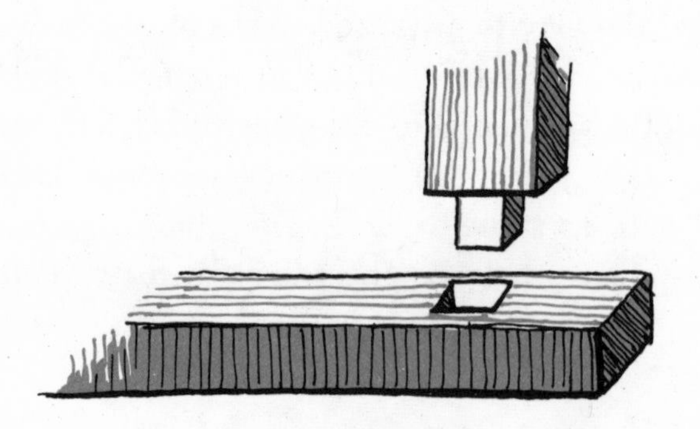

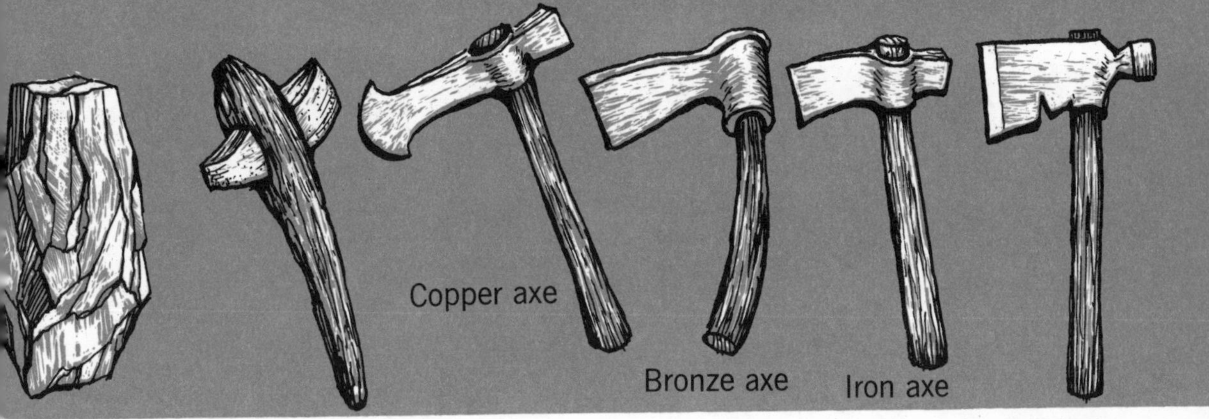

THE HAND AXE: FROM THE OLD STONE AGE TO THE PRESENT

The Coming of Metals

LITTLE was known about metals in the New Stone Age. Occasionally men picked up small nuggets of pure gold or silver and used the mysterious shiny stones for ornaments. Most metals, however, do not exist in the pure form. They are usually found combined with other elements in a mixture of minerals called an *ore*.

The Age of Metals began with gleaming red copper – the first pure metal that man separated from its ore.

When powdered copper ore is heated with charcoal, the copper is released from the elements with which it was combined and is purified. This *smelting* process, discovered about 4000 B.C., was the key to the earth's treasury of metals. Sometimes the words *smelt* and *melt* are confused. The purpose of smelting is to remove the pure metal from the ore. The purpose of melting is to change

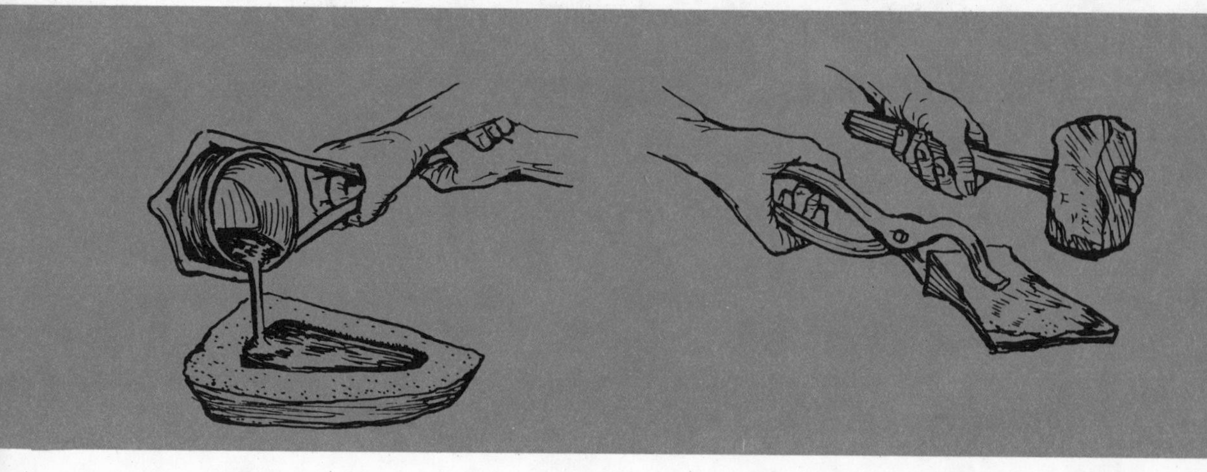

Axe heads cast from liquid copper   Hammering metal into shape

a solid to a liquid. For example, solid copper that is heated to a temperature of 2000° F. will become liquid just as ice does when heated above 32° F.

Tools were made by pouring liquid copper into molds of clay or stone. After the copper solidified into the desired shape, it was removed from the mold and hardened by hammering. Sharp edges were then ground on the hardened knives, axes, and other cutting tools. Up to the time that the process for making bronze was discovered, copper remained the only metal for making tools.

When copper is mixed with tin, the alloy called *bronze* is formed. An *alloy* is a mixture of two or more metals. The amounts of these metals can be varied to give different *properties* to the alloy. For example, more tin will make bronze harder. But too much tin will make bronze brittle and easy to chip. During the Bronze Age, which started about 3000 B.C., a mixture of one part of tin and nine parts of copper produced the best bronze alloy for tools. This combination is better than copper for making tools; it is harder, stronger, and can be molded more easily.

The toolmaker's trade flourished in the Bronze Age. The newly-found alloy was turned into axes and chisels, spearheads, daggers and swords, and saws, drills and files for woodworking.

The Iron Age started about 1200 B.C. Over the next few hundred years, bronze and stone were slowly abandoned and iron took their place. Bronze was an expensive metal with many good qualities. But iron was tougher and harder. It provided superior tools for all.

Most of the tools that can be found in a modern tool kit were also produced during the Iron Age. During this time new tools were invented and old ones were improved. Toolmakers of the

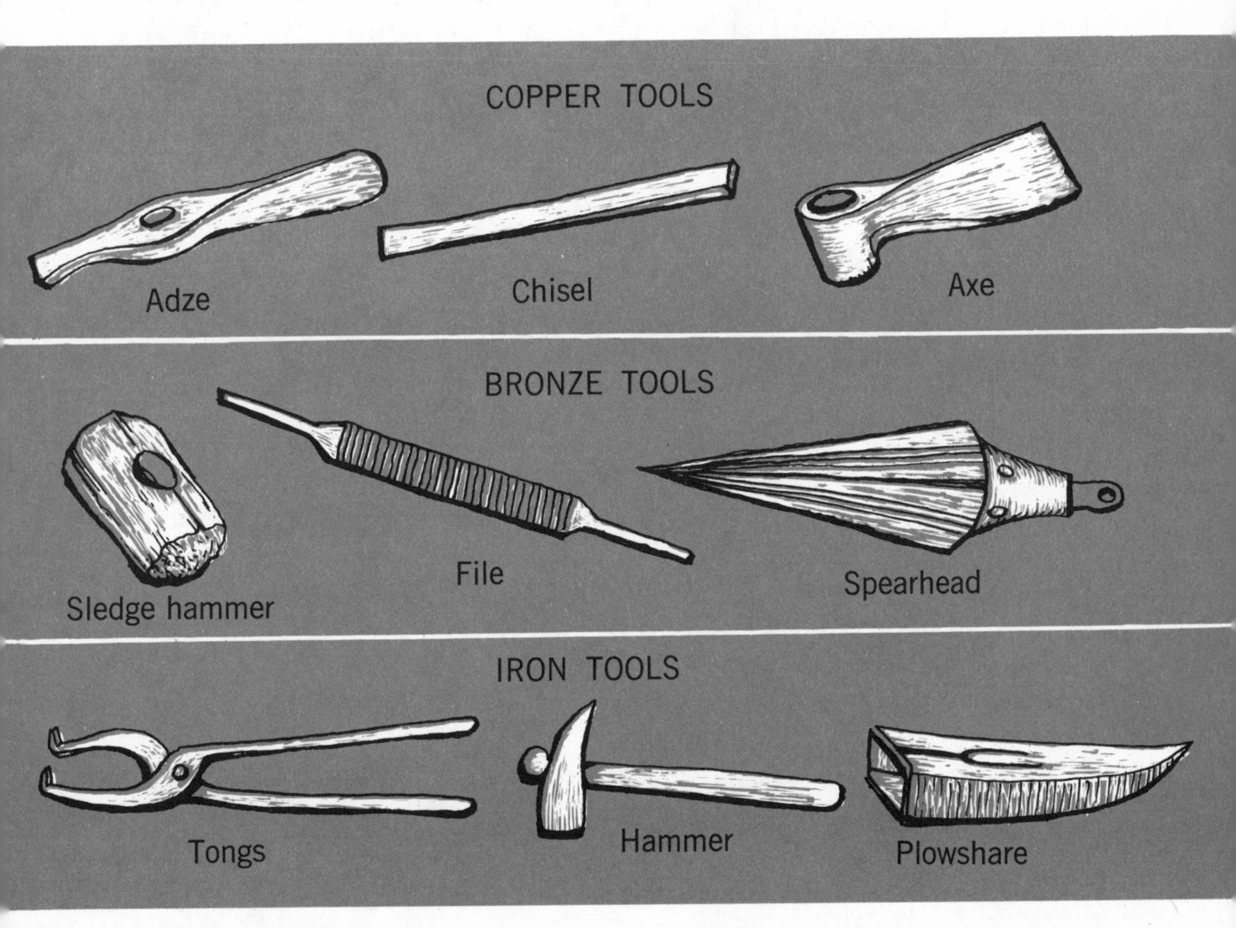

Iron Age gave the world hinged tongs for gripping hot objects, forms for making nails, shears for cutting the wool from sheep, the hacksaw, and blocks with holes for drawing hot iron through them to form wire. Special drills and hammers were designed for different crafts, and the new chisels and files of hard iron made metalworking more successful. Iron axes bit deep into trees, turning whole forests into cleared farm land. Plowshares grooved the soil to receive seeds. Hoes, spades, and shovels of iron were introduced. Agriculture progressed and the work of the farmer became easier.

There are three kinds of iron, all containing different amounts of the element carbon. The carbon comes from the charcoal in the smelting fire.

Wrought iron contains little or no carbon. It is tough but too soft to produce good cutting edges. *Cast iron* contains the most carbon of the three types. Although it is very hard, cast iron is too brittle to be used for tools. *Steel* is an in-between metal. It has more carbon than wrought iron and less carbon than cast iron. The properties of steel are a good compromise of both extremes.

The metalworkers of the Iron Age produced steels by increasing the amount of carbon in wrought iron. *Tempering* and *quenching* were also developed by these ancient metal smiths. Steels are tempered — heated and slowly cooled — to improve their toughness. They are quenched — heated and suddenly cooled by immersion in cold water — to improve their hardness.

Since the days of the Iron Age, steel has always been the most desirable form of iron for making tools.

From Generation to Generation

THE MATERIALS out of which tools are made have changed and improved over thousands of years. Wood is still important for tool handles, but stone, bone, and to a great degree bronze, have given way to steel and plastic.

Yet if craftsmen from the Old Stone Age, the New Stone Age, and ancient Egypt could visit a modern hardware store, they would recognize many of the tools on the shelves. The resemblance between the tools of these long dead craftsmen and those of today show that when men of different periods experience the same problems, they frequently work out similar solutions.

Because tools help us to achieve the high purpose of improving our lives, they are regarded as one of the great heritages that people pass on to the generations that follow them.

The glory that tools give to man is that they allow him to cut, saw, pound, and build his way to a better world. The direction of man's growth, his hopes for freedom and happiness, and his eventual conquests of atomic power and space all had their dim start a million years ago when he descended from the trees. It was then that he began his journey toward civilization. But without man's inborn ability to use and later to make tools, the journey would have been impossible. For tools helped man gain his first and most necessary triumph: victory over the savage life of his ancestors.

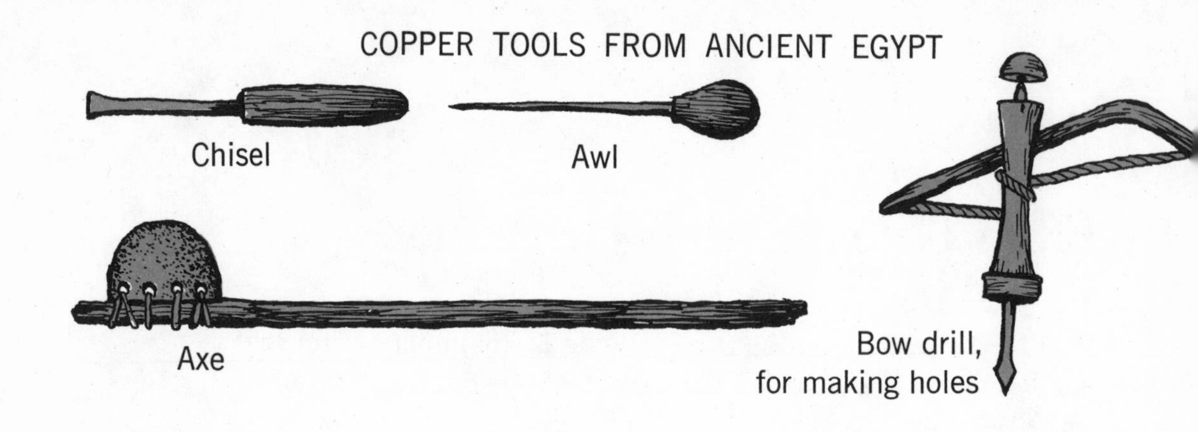
COPPER TOOLS FROM ANCIENT EGYPT
Chisel
Awl
Axe
Bow drill,
for making holes

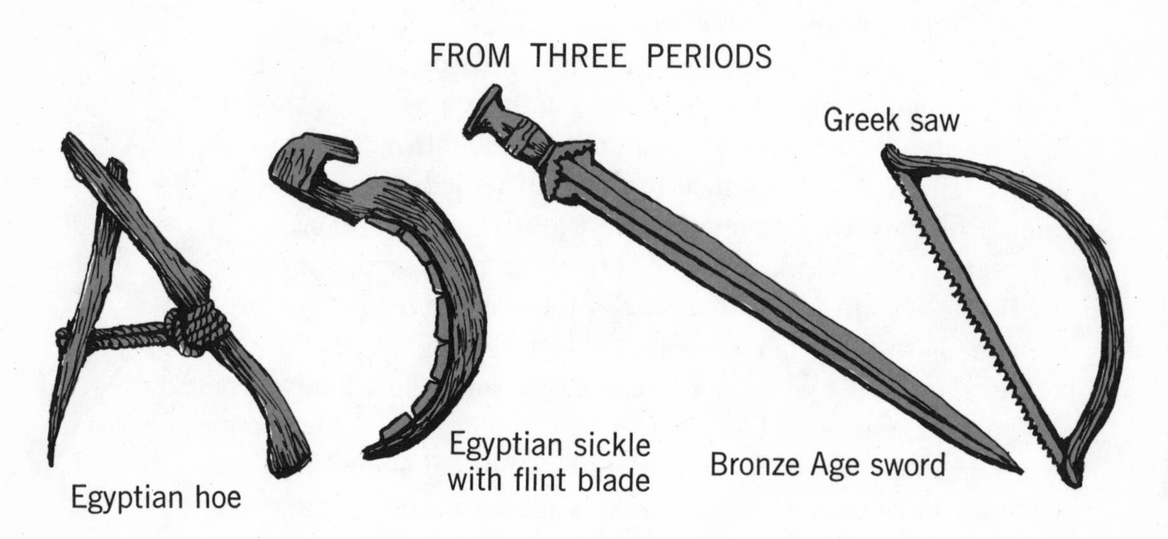
FROM THREE PERIODS
Greek saw
Egyptian hoe
Egyptian sickle
with flint blade
Bronze Age sword

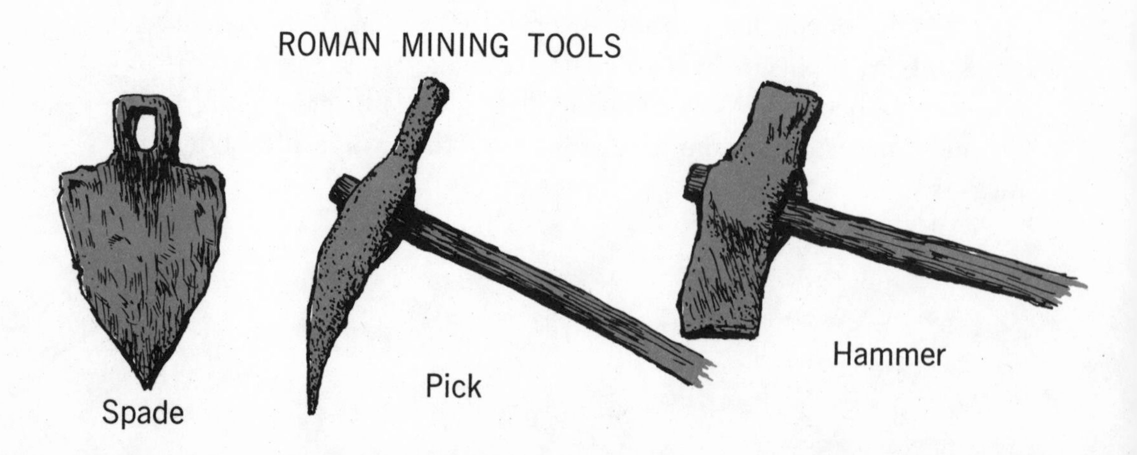
ROMAN MINING TOOLS
Spade
Pick
Hammer

ROMAN WOODWORKING TOOLS

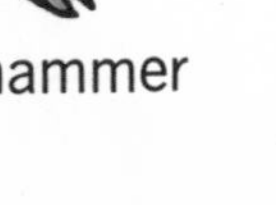

Special Words

Alloy: a mixture of two or more metals, for example, bronze (copper and tin) and brass (copper and zinc).

Bronze Age: a period in man's history that started about 4000 B. C. and ended about 1200 B.C., when the Iron Age started.

Cro Magnon: a race of men that lived about 30,000 years ago. They decorated their caves and tools with beautiful paintings and sculptures.

Environment: surroundings that influence growth and development.

Flint: a hard and brittle stone used by early men to make tools.

Force: any push or pull.

Friction: the resistance that is produced when one object rubs against another object.

Fulcrum: the point on which a lever turns.

Iron Age: a period in man's history that started about 1200 B.C. Some people say that the Iron Age has never ended and we are still living in it. Others call our period the Steel Age, the Atomic Age, the Jet Age, or the Space Age.

Loom: a device for weaving cloth.

Machine: a complicated device for doing work. Machines are operated by outside energy, like electricity, gasoline, or the atom.

Mechanical Advantage: the number of times that the load is greater than the force that is applied to the machine.

Melting: heating a solid until it turns to a liquid.

New Stone Age: a period in man's history that started between 7000 to 11,000 years ago and ended about 4000 B.C., when the Bronze Age started.

Ore: a mixture of minerals that contains at least one valuable metal.

Potter's Wheel: a flat, revolving disk on which clay is shaped for pottery.

Pottery: any object that is molded out of clay and then hardened by fire.

Quenching: heating and rapidly cooling a metal to improve its hardness.

Simple Machines: devices that make work easier. The six simple machines are the lever, the pulley, the wheel and axle, the inclined plane, the wedge, and the screw.

Smelting: a heating process that removes pure metal from its ore.

Spindle: a revolving stick or rod used for spinning and winding thread.

Spinning: twisting fibers together to make thread.

Tempering: heating and slowly cooling a metal to improve its toughness.

Tools: simple instruments for doing work. The energy to operate a tool is supplied by the body. Most tools are combinations or variations of the simple machines.

Weaving: making cloth by having the threads that go in one direction travel over and under the threads that go in the other direction.

Work: in science, the force needed to move an object multiplied by the distance that the object moves.

Index

Adze, 48
Alloy, 50, 56
Animals:
  man's superiority over, 12-13, 37
  tool-using, 13
  vision of, 16
Antler, use of, in ancient tools, 40, 43
Archimedes, *quoted,* 24
Arm, human, 28
Axes, 17, 33, 52
  in Bronze Age, 51
  first metal, 50
  in New Stone Age, 48

Basket weaving, 45-46
Bone, use of, for ancient tools, 40, 42, 43, 44
Bronze:
  properties of, 50-51
  use of, during Bronze Age, 51
Bronze Age, 24, 50-51, 56
  tools of, 51

Capstan, 31
Cast iron, 52
Chert, use of, for ancient tools, 41
Chisels, 17, 33, 52
  in Bronze Age, 51
  of New Stone Age, 48
Copper:
  first metal used for tools, 49-50
  superseded by bronze, 50-51
Corkscrew, 34
Covering tools, 21
Cro-Magnon men, 42-43, 56
Crowbar, 28
Cutting tools, 17
  smooth-edged, 19
  tooth-edged, 18

Doorknobs, 31
Digging tools, 17
Drilling, 37
Drills, 52
  in Bronze Age, 51

Emerson, Ralph Waldo, *quoted,* 45

Files, 17, 52
  in Bronze Age, 51
Fire, making, ancient method of, 43
Fishing pole, 28
Flint:
  characteristics of, 40, 56
  mining of, in New Stone Age, 41
  striking fire with, 43
  use of, in New Stone Age, 43-44
  use of, in Old Stone Age, 40, 43

Foot-pounds, work unit, 24
Force, *defined*, 25, 56
Friction, 28, 56
Fulcrum, 28-29
  defined, 56

Gangplanks, 32
Gathering tools, 23
Grinding, 37, 45, 47-48
  invented in Old Stone Age, 44
  in New Stone Age, 44-45, 47-48
Gripping tools, 22

Hacksaw, 52
Hammers, 17, 37, 52
Hand, human:
  construction of, 14-16
  as tool of early man, 11, 14
Handles, 42, 53
Hoes, 52
  in New Stone Age, 44

Ideal machines, *defined*, 28
Inclined plane, 24, 31-33
  examples of, 32
  special forms of, 33, 34
Iron:
  beginning of use of, 51
  kinds of, 52
  replaces other materials, 53
Iron Age, 24, 51-52, 56
  tools of, 51-52
Ivory, use of, in ancient tools, 40, 43

Jackscrew, 24, 34
Joining tools, 21

Knives, 17, 33, 37
  first metal, 50
  of New Stone Age, 48

Lever, 17, 24, 28-30, 37
  classes of, 29
  examples of, 28, 29
Lifting tools, 22
Log-wheels, 36
Loom:
  defined, 56
  of New Stone Age, 46

Machines:
  defined, 16, 56
  ideal, 28
  simple, 17, 24-34, 57
Man:
  natural tools of, 11, 17
  superiority of, over animals, 12-13, 37
  three-dimensional vision of, 16
  from user to maker of tools, 38-40
Materials for tools, 53
  alloys, 50-51
  bone, 40, 42, 43, 44, 53
  bronze, 50-51, 53
  copper, 50
  iron, 51-52
  metals, 49-52
  plastic, 53
  primitive, 40, 41
  steel, 52, 53
  stone, 40-41, 51, 53
  wood, 40, 41-42, 44, 53
Mechanical advantage:
  defined: 26, 56
  of inclined plane, 32
  of levers, 30
  of pulleys, 26
  of wheel and axle, 31
Melting, *defined*, 49-50, 56
Metals:
  alloys of, 50, 56
  copper, 49-50
  form found in, in nature, 49
  iron, 51-52
  smelting of, 49, 57
  steel, 52
Metals, Age of, 49. *See also* Bronze Age; Iron Age

Mortar and pestle, 44-45
Mortise and tenon, *defined,* 48
Moving and lifting tools, 22

Nails, 33, 52
New Stone Age, 24, 43-48, 56
  changes in way of life in, 43, 45
  cloth-making in, 46-47
  farming tools of, 43-44
  flint mining in, 41
  grinding methods in, 44-45, 47-48
  use and making of containers in, 45-46, 47
  use of metals in, 49
  woodworking in, 48
Nut and bolt, 34

Obsidian, use of, for ancient tools, 41
Old Stone Age, 11-12, 37-43
  grinding in, 44
  materials used in, 40, 41
  origin of name of, 41
  rope-making in, 42
  toolmaking in, 39-40, 42-43
Ore, *defined,* 49, 57

Pencil sharpener, 31
Pestle, mortar and, 44-45
Piercing tools, 19
Plane, inclined, 24, 31-33
  examples of, 32
  special forms of, 33, 34
Plastic, 53
Plowshares, 52
Potter's wheel, 34-35, 57
Pottery, 35, 47, 57
Pounding tools, 17, 18
Power tools, *defined,* 16. *See also* Machines
Pulley, 24, 26-27

Quenching, *defined,* 52, 57

Ramps, 32
Rope-making, ancient, 42, 46
Rotating tools, 23

Saddle quern, 45
Sandpaper, 17
Saws, 16, 17, 52
  in Bronze Age, 51
Scissors, 29
Screw jack, 24, 34
Screws, 24, 34
Seesaw, 28
Shafts, 42
Shearing tools, 20
Shears, 52
Shell, use of, in ancient tools, 40, 43
Shovels, 17, 37, 52
Simple machines, 17, 24-34, 57
  inclined plane, 31-33
  levers, 28-30
  pulleys, 26-27
  screws, 34
  wedges, 33
  wheel and axle, 31
Smelting:
  defined, 57
  discovery of process of, 49
  vs. melting, 49-50
Smooth edge cutting tools, 19
Solid wheels, 36
Spades, 17, 52
Spears, 17, 37, 51
Spinning, 37, 57
  ancient method, 42
  in New Stone Age, 46
Spoked wheels, 36
Stairways, 32
Steel, 52, 53
Steering wheel, 31
Stone, use of, in ancient tools, 40-41
Stone Age. *See* New Stone Age; Old Stone Age
Surface-scraping tools, 17, 20

Teeth, as natural tool, 11, 17

Tempering, *defined,* 52, 57
Tongs, 29, 52
Toolmaking:
  ancient materials for, 40
  beginning of use of metals in, 50
  beginnings of, 39-40
  in Bronze Age, 51
  of Cro-Magnon men, 42-43
  in Iron Age, 51-52
  modern materials for, 53
  in New Stone Age, 43-44, 47-48
  in Old Stone Age, 39-40, 42-43
Tools:
  defined, 16, 57
  discovery of, in ancient times, 37-39
  groups of, 17-24
  moving in circles, 34-37
  nature of, 17
  power, 16
Toothed cutting tools, 18
Transportation, 34-35, 36
Tweezers, 29

Vise, 34

Weapons, 17, 51
Weaving:
  defined, 57
  invention of, 46-47
Wedge, 17, 24, 33
Wheel and axle, 24, 31
Wheels:
  importance of, 34-35
  log-wheels, 36
  potter's, 35
  solid, 36
  spoked, 36
  steering, 31
Whitman, Walt, *quoted,* 15
Windlass, 31
Wire, making, 52
Wood, use of:
  for ancient tools, 40, 41-42, 44
  for modern tools, 53
  progress of, in New Stone Age, 48
Wood screw, 34
Work, in science:
  defined, 25, 57
  law of, 28
  measuring unit of, 24-25
Wrought iron, 52

FIRST BOOKS

classified by subject

Some titles are listed in more than one category

The ARTS

Architecture
Ballet
Bells
Color
Drawing
Gardening
How to Fix It
Jazz
Music
Paintings
Photography
Poetry
Puppets
Rhythms
Stage Costume and Make-Up

COMMUNICATIONS

Atlas
Codes and Ciphers
Language & How To Use It
Letter Writing
Maps and Globes
Measurement
Printing
Public Libraries
Teaching Machines
Television
Words

SCIENCE

Air
Airplanes
Antarctic
Archaeology
Architecture
Astronomy
Automobiles
Bees
Bells
Birds
Bridges
Bugs
Caves
Color
Conservation
Cotton
Earth
Electricity
Food
Glaciers
Glass
Human Senses
Light
Machines
Mammals
Maps and Globes
Measurement
Microbes
Mining
Ocean
Photography
Plants
Prehistoric Animals
Rhythms
Roads
Science Experiments
Sea Shells
Snakes
Sound
Space Travel
Stone Age Man
Stones
Submarines
Television
Tools
Trains
Trees
Tropical Mammals
Water
Weather
Wild Flowers

SPORTS & HOBBIES

Baseball
Basketball
Boys' Cooking
Cartoons for Kids
Cats
Chess
Christmas Joy
Codes and Ciphers
Dogs
Dolls
Football
Gardening
Horses
How to Fix It
Jokes
Magic
Photography
Physical Fitness
Sailing
Stones
Surprising Facts
Swimming

SOCIAL STUDIES

United States

Atlas
American History
American Revolution
California Gold Rush
The China Clippers
Civil War Land Battles
Civil War Naval Actions
Congress
Constitution
Early Settlers
Hawaii
Holidays
Indian Wars
Indians
National Monuments
National Parks
Negroes
New England
New World Explorers
Oregon Trail
Panama Canal
Pioneers
Presidents
Supreme Court
United Nations
War of 1812
Washington, D.C.
World War I
World War II

The World About Us

Africa
Ancient Bible Lands
Ancient Egypt
Ancient Mesopotamia and Persia
Ancient Greece
Ancient Rome
Antarctic
Archaeology
Australia
Barbarian Invaders
Brazil
Canada
Communist China
Congo
England
Eskimos
Festivals
France
Ghana
India
Israel
Italy
Japan
Kings
Medieval Man
Mediterranean
Mexico
Netherlands
New Zealand
Ocean
Pakistan
South America
Soviet Union
United Nations
Vikings
West Germany
West Indies
World War I
World War II

People and Products

Conservation
Cotton
Cowboys
Firemen
Food
Glass
Nurses
Supermarkets
Water

LITERATURE & LANGUAGE ARTS

Codes and Ciphers
Color
Fairy Tales
Language & How To Use It
Letter Writing
Legendary Beings
Maps and Globes
Mythology
Mythical Beasts
Norse Legends
Poetry
Printing
Teaching Machines
Words

TRANSPORTATION

Airplanes
Automobiles
Boats
Bridges
Maps and Globes
Panama Canal
Roads
Ships
Space Travel
Trains
Water